MASTER THE ART OF DIGITAL MARKETING

THE BEST ONLINE MARKETING STRATEGIES TO MAKE YOU THE MOST MONEY IN HALF THE TIME

AMELIA KOONJBEHARRY

CONTENTS

INTRODUCTION

Welcome to the revolution; you are about to enter the digital marketing game; are you ready? Where the opportunities are endless and on the rise, and the only limits are the ones you place on yourself. In this era, mastering digital marketing isn't just a skill—it's your ticket to a lifestyle of freedom, flexibility, and financial independence. It's where dreams of traveling the world, running a successful online business, and escaping the 9-5 grind become reality. It's not just about being online; it's about leveraging the digital world to create a life you love on your terms!

My goal in writing this book is clear: to guide you toward achieving financial independence through the power of digital marketing. I'm here to offer you not just theories but actionable knowledge, up-to-date strategies for 2024 specifically, and real-life applications that have worked for me and countless others. This book is about understanding digital marketing as more than a set of tools—it's about embracing a lifestyle that gives you the freedom to work from anywhere, the flexibility to set your schedule, and the potential to create multiple income streams.

This book is structured in two main parts. First, it takes you through the adventure of starting an online business from scratch—think of it as your foundation. Then, we'll dive into growing and scaling that business, turning a foundation into a thriving empire. Along the way, you'll encounter case studies, step-by-step guides, and insights into niche selection. Every piece of advice is geared towards practical, actionable results, giving you the reassurance and guidance you need.

Who is this book for? It's tailored for those eager to blend travel, work, and financial independence into one seamless lifestyle. It's for dreamers who refuse to settle for a traditional 9-5 job and opt to build a life filled with multiple income streams online. You're not just looking for a career, but a life that excites and fulfills you.

Expect this book to be your roadmap in the digital marketing world, preparing you with the tools and knowledge needed to thrive. However, remember that the journey to success is paved with dedication, adaptability, and an unyielding willingness to apply the strategies we discuss. And if I may add one of my favorites, it's the ability to show up with consistent resilience, always remembering your "why."

As we start this journey together, I invite you to envision the boundless possibilities that mastering digital marketing can unlock. Picture a life where work and play blur into one. Financial freedom is not just a dream but your daily reality, and you are the captain of your soul. Let this book be your boarding pass on the flight we're about to take.

-Amelia Koonjbeharry

CHAPTER 1
LAYING OUR FOUNDATION

The field of digital marketing, where threads of technology, creativity, and strategy are interwoven, holds the potential for unparalleled freedom and success. Yet, navigating this intricate field demands more than a detailed understanding of tools and trends; it calls for a deep dive into the psychology that fuels a digital marketer's relentless drive. The essence of this journey begins not with external strategies alone but with an introspection into the motivations, resilience, adaptability, and visions that shape your path.

1.1 THE PSYCHOLOGY OF A SUCCESSFUL DIGITAL MARKER

Every digital marketer's journey is underscored by a unique 'why'—a powerful force that propels them forward. This 'why' is not just a fleeting thought, but a beacon that guides them through the tumultuous array of industry changes and challenges. It might be the longing for autonomy, the desire to impact the world, or the pursuit of creative expression. Whatever it is, recognizing and embracing this 'why' aligns your career with your life's values and ambitions, creating a harmonious existence where work feels less like an obligation and more like a purposeful endeavor.

In this space, change is the only constant. Algorithms shift, platforms evolve, and audience preferences fluctuate dizzily. Herein lies the importance of mental resilience—a quality that enables marketers to view setbacks not as insurmountable obstacles but as stepping stones to more significant achievements. Developing this resilience involves cultivating a mindset that thrives on challenges, learns from failures, and remains unfazed by the rapid pace of change. It's about building an inner fortitude that supports your ambitions, ensuring that your resolve gets more challenging when it gets tricky.

Much like resilience, adaptability is a cornerstone of success in digital marketing. It's the ability to pivot strategies, embrace new platforms, and understand emerging audience behaviors while maintaining the essence of your marketing approach. This agility is akin to a surfer skillfully riding the waves—regardless of their size or speed, the surfer remains in control, navigating each wave with finesse and determination. Adaptability means staying abreast of industry trends, experimenting with new ideas, and letting go of tactics that no longer serve your goals. It's the duo between flexibility and steadfastness, where agility meets strategy.

Lastly, the journey through the digital marketing world is not a sprint but a marathon, requiring a vision that extends far out. Long-term visioning is about setting sights on future goals while appreciating the steps needed. It's understanding that success is not an overnight phenomenon but the result of consistent effort, strategic planning, and an unwavering commitment to your goals. This vision acts as a compass, guiding actions today while clarifying your aspirations. It's about dreaming big but planning meticulously, ensuring that each step you take is a calculated move toward your ultimate destination.

Reflective Exercise: Crafting Your Digital Marketing Blueprint

Take a moment to reflect on your 'why,' resilience, adaptability, and long-term vision. Grab a notebook or open a digital document and consider the following prompts:

1. Your 'Why': Write down what drew you into digital marketing. How does this align with your personal values and lifestyle aspirations?
2. Resilience Building: Consider a recent setback or challenge in your digital marketing efforts. How did you respond? What did you learn, and how can you apply this lesson to build greater resilience?
3. Adaptability in Action: Reflect on a time when you had to adapt your strategy due to a change in the digital landscape. What was the outcome? How did this experience enhance your adaptability skills?
4. Vision for the Future: Envision where you'd like to be in your digital marketing career five years from now. What steps do you need to take to make this vision a reality?

This exercise is not just about introspection; it's a strategic tool for mapping out your path in digital marketing, ensuring that your professional endeavors are deeply intertwined with your aspirations and strengths.

1.2 THE IMPORTANCE OF A GROWTH MINDSET

It would help to consider the significance of fostering a growth mindset in this field. This mindset, characterized by an eagerness to expand one's capabilities and resilience in the face of challenges, is the backbone on which marketers build their careers. Rather than being seen as insurmountable obstacles, challenges are embraced as opportunities for growth, pushing the boundaries of what is possible and leading to innovative solutions that set trends rather than follow them.

A growth mindset thrives on the notion that abilities and intelligence form through dedication and hard work. This perspective shifts the focus from fearing failure to celebrating learning, encouraging marketers to get out of their familiar zones and play around with new strategies, tools, and ideas. With its rapid technological advancements and shifting consumer behaviors, the digital marketing sphere demands such an approach. Marketers who seek out challenges find themselves at the forefront of the industry, capable of leveraging emerging trends and technologies to their advantage.

Continuous learning is the fuel that propels individuals with a growth mindset. In an industry where yesterday's innovative strategies can quickly become today's outdated tactics, committing to lifelong learning is not just beneficial; it's necessary. This commitment might manifest in various forms, from enrolling in the highest ticket online courses, attending industry conferences, dedicating weekly time to reading the latest digital marketing publications, and experimenting with new marketing tools and platforms. Creating a personal development plan provides structure to this learning process, ensuring that pursuing knowledge is intentional and aligned with one's career goals. This plan is the roadmap, guiding marketers to remain adaptable and informed.

Feedback loops play a pivotal role in cultivating a growth mindset. In digital marketing, feedback can come from multiple sources: peers offering insights into your strategies, mentors sharing wisdom and experiences, and even the audience responding to your campaigns. Implementing systems to collect and analyze this feedback regularly is crucial. It may involve conducting surveys, monitoring social media interactions, or establishing regular check-ins with mentors and colleagues. This feedback provides invaluable insights into areas of strength and opportunities for improvement, enabling marketers to refine their approaches and better meet the needs of their audience. It's a cycle of learning, applying, receiving feedback, and iterating, which fosters continuous improvement and innovation.

Celebrating progress, no matter how small, is vital to maintaining consistency within a growth mindset framework. In the fast-paced world of digital marketing, where goals can be lofty and the pressure to succeed is high, it's easy to overlook the small victories. However, acknowledging and celebrating these milestones is essential for sustaining the drive and consistency over the long term. It could be as simple as a successful A/B test that led to increased engagement, a viral social media campaign, or even acquiring a new skill or certification. Recognizing these achievements reinforces the value of the learning process and the incremental gains that lead to significant success. It serves as a reminder that progress in digital marketing is not always linear and that every incremental stride, regardless of size, moves us closer to our goal.

In the world of digital marketing, where change is the only constant, embracing a growth mindset is imperative. This outlook sees challenges as opportunities, values continuous learning and feedback, and celebrates each step forward. This approach ensures that one remains resilient, adaptable, and innovative, ready to navigate and emerge successful.

1.3 BUILDING DISCIPLINE WHILE KEEPING FLEXIBLE

This space is relentlessly pacey and in high demand, so cultivating discipline is critical. Structured flexibility, then, becomes the backbone of managing the appropriate attributes. It involves setting routines that are not cast in iron but are fluid enough to adapt to unforeseen changes, allowing digital marketers to navigate their day with a sense of purpose and direction. This could mean dedicating mornings to creative tasks when the mind is fresh while leaving afternoons for meetings and administrative work, with the understanding that this structure can bend as necessary. The key lies in creating a framework within which flexibility is not just allowed but is a built-in feature.

The art of prioritizing tasks stands at the forefront of maintaining this balance between discipline and flexibility. It requires a keen eye to sift through many functions and pinpoint urgent and important ones. This prioritization is not merely about listing tasks but about understanding their impact on broader goals, enabling digital marketers to navigate their days not just with efficiency but with strategic intent. It's about recognizing that not all tasks are created equal and that focusing on the right ones at the right time can propel one's objectives forward more effectively than attempting to tackle everything simultaneously. Your profit-generating activities should be the highest priority on the list of tasks for the day!

In this digital age, tools and applications designed for remote work are in abundance of this disciplined yet flexible approach. From time trackers that offer insights into how hours are spent to project management apps that keep teams synced regardless of their physical locations, these tools are the core of keeping everything in an appropriate flow. They provide structure, streamline workflows, and ensure that even when the work environment is fluid, deadlines are met, and productivity levels are maintained. Utilizing these tools is not just about staying organized; it's about creating an environment where discipline and flexibility coexist, enabling marketers to meet the demands of their roles without falling victim to chaos.

With all this balancing comes the importance of mindfulness and self-care. Simply put, there is no room to exclude this. In a profession where burnout is right around the corner, incorporating practices that nurture the mind, body, and spirit is not just beneficial; it's essential. With its roots in being present and fully engaged at the moment, mindfulness offers a counterbalance to the relentless pace, providing a space for clarity and focus amidst the whirlwind of tasks and deadlines. Self-care acts as a foundation for sustainable productivity. Whether in the form of regular physical activity, hobbies that disconnect one from one's devices, or ensuring adequate rest. It's a reminder that in the pursuit of becoming a digital master, the well-being of the marketers cannot be compromised; instead, it's a part of their daily routine.

The relationship between discipline and flexibility is manageable by incorporating prioritization and simply leveraging the digital tools at our fingertips. It's critical to understand that productivity is not about rigidly adhering to plans but about navigating the day with intention, adaptability, and a mindful approach to one's well-being. Abiding by this simple formula can provide the structure for innovation to flourish.

1.4 OVERCOMING THE FEAR OF FAILURE

In the dynamic world of digital marketing, failure can hang around, casting a shadow over even the most ambitious endeavors. Yet, the true sign of a seasoned marketer lies not in a clear track record but in the ability to transform failure into a catalyst for growth and innovation. This process begins with a fundamental shift in perspective, where setbacks are not viewed as defeats but as invaluable lessons that pave the way to success. This reframing of failure necessitates a deep understanding that every misstep unveils new insights, pushing the boundaries of creativity and leading to groundbreaking strategies that reshape the digital landscape. As cliche as it sounds, failure can often be a real blessing in disguise here.

Taking calculated risks then stands as the cornerstone of navigating. It involves an assessment of potential outcomes, where the focus shifts from the fear of losing to the potential for breakthroughs. This approach requires an understanding of distinguishing between reckless gambles and strategic ventures, recognizing that the most significant triumphs often emerge from the willingness to venture into unfamiliar territories. The calculus of risk-taking thus becomes an art form, balancing the potential for loss against the promise of significant rewards. It's an intricate process where each step is guided by thorough research, informed intuition, and just true belief in the vision that propels one forward.

Amidst the challenges and uncertainties, the value of a support network can be crucial for consistently persevering. As you may be fraught with hurdles and setbacks, you must surround yourself with mentors and coaching groups who can provide new perspectives to ensure constant growth. These relationships foster a sense of belonging and resilience, offering a safety net that cushions a potential fall and propels one back into their state of creativity. With their wealth of experience and insight, a mentor acts as a beacon of light, guiding through the darkest moments and offering strategies to navigate complex challenges. Similarly, a community of like-minded individuals offers solace and inspiration, reminding us that the path is shared and that setbacks are universal stepping stones toward mastery.

Crafting a failure recovery plan emerges as the final piece of the puzzle, ensuring a swift and efficient comeback from setbacks. This plan outlines clear steps to assess the situation, extract lessons, and recalibrate strategies after failure. It emphasizes the importance of maintaining a solution-oriented mindset, which focuses steadfastly on forward movement and growth. This involves thoroughly analyzing what went awry and a systematic strategy to tackle root causes and prevent future missteps. The failure recovery plan serves as a roadmap, guiding through the aftermath of a setback with precision and purpose, ensuring that each failure does not take one out but instead serves as a slight detour.

In this relentless pursuit of becoming a digital marketing success, the interplay between reframing failure, embracing calculated risks, nurturing a supportive network, and implementing a failure recovery plan forms the most solid framework possible. It underscores a fundamental truth: when confronted and harnessed, the fear of failure transforms into a powerful force that propels one toward unprecedented success. Through this lens, failure ceases to be an endpoint; it becomes a crucial ingredient in the alchemy of digital marketing mastery, where setbacks are not merely endured but celebrated as harbingers of breakthroughs and innovation.

1.5 SETTING REALISTIC GOALS AND EXPECTATIONS

Goal setting is not just another item to check off a list; it is a compass that guides your strategies, decisions, and actions. It starts with the craft of setting SMART goals—objectives that are Specific, Measurable, Achievable, Relevant, and Time-bound. This method ensures that your ambitions are not just castles built in the air but are based on what is achievable within reality within a given timeframe with available resources. For instance, rather than aiming vaguely to "increase social media engagement," a SMART goal would specify "to increase Instagram engagement by 20% within three months by implementing a new content strategy," making the goal clear, trackable, and bounded by time.

Benchmarking success takes this a step further by placing your goals within the broader landscape of your industry and your past performance. It involves a meticulous analysis, where data acts as the lens through which you gauge the effectiveness of your strategies against your competition and your historical achievements. This process could reveal that a 20% increase in engagement is not just a personal victory but also surpasses industry norms, providing a dual sense of accomplishment and strategic insight. Benchmarking, thus, serves as a mirror, reflecting where you stand in the grand scheme and how far you have journeyed, grounding your aspirations in the context of the broader digital marketing ecosystem.

Understanding that this market is constantly changing, influenced by emerging trends, platform algorithm updates, and shifting consumer behaviors. This dynamism necessitates the flexibility to adjust your goals as new information comes to light. Such adjustments are not admissions of defeat but are acknowledgments of the evolving nature of the digital realm. They require an ongoing relationship with data, where analytics inform strategic pivots and ensure your goals remain aligned with the current state of play. For example, if an algorithm change drastically reduces your content's reach, revising your engagement goals to reflect this new reality is not just prudent; it's vital for maintaining momentum and focusing your efforts where they can have the most impact.

Balancing ambition with realism is the most delicate aspect of setting goals in digital marketing. On one hand, ambition fuels progress, pushing you to reach heights you might have thought unattainable. Conversely, without a grounding in realism, ambition can set you on a path toward burnout and disillusionment. The key lies in setting goals that stretch your capabilities without straying into impossibility. It's about recognizing the difference between what is challenging yet achievable with effort and dedication and what is a setup for failure. This balance prevents the cycle of setting overly ambitious goals, failing to meet them, and facing discouragement. Instead, it fosters a cycle of achievement, satisfaction, and increased motivation; for digital marketers, this might mean setting progressively more challenging goals, each building on the success of the last rather than a single, monumental goal that seems impossible from the start.

Navigating the balance between ambition and realism also involves being aware of the signs of burnout or fatigue and taking proactive steps to mitigate them. Digital marketing, with its relentless pace and constant demand for innovation, can be as exhausting as it is exhilarating. Recognizing the toll this can take on your mental and physical health is crucial. It means understanding that sometimes, slowing down to recharge is not a setback but a strategic move that ensures you can continue to pursue your goals with vigor. It's about listening to your body, mind, and spirit, acknowledging when you're pushing too hard, and allowing yourself the time and space needed to recover. This approach ensures that your pursuit of goals is sustainable over the long term, maintaining a pace that keeps you engaged and excited about your work without edging into burnout.

In this intricate play of setting and pursuing goals, the interplay between ambition, realism, and the strategic adjustment of objectives forms the foundation of sustained success and well-being. This process demands both vigilance and flexibility and a willingness to push boundaries while recognizing the importance of balance and self-care. Through this process, goals become more than targets to achieve; they become stepping stones on a path that is not just about professional achievement but also personal growth and fulfillment.

CHAPTER 2

CARVING YOUR NICHE IN THE DIGITAL TERRAIN

The question "What is my niche?" is relevant in this marketing space! The concept of a niche serves as both your compass and your map, guiding you to where your enthusiasm meets the market's demands in harmonious profitability. It's not about fitting into a predefined box but shaping a space where your unique voice resonates with a specific audience, creating ripples that become waves of influence and success.

2.1 IDENTIFYING YOUR PASSION AND AUDIENCE

Passion Meets Market Needs

Fusing personal interests with market needs is akin to a chef crafting a new dish. Just as a chef combines ingredients in a way that appeals to the palate of their diners, you must blend your passions with what the market craves. This synergy ensures the viability of your niche and infuses your work with an authenticity that attracts and retains an engaged audience. It's about asking yourself, "What do I love?" and then, "Who else loves this, and how can I serve them?"

Understanding Your Audience

Diving deep into audience demographics, psychographics, and pain points is crucial to ensure your niche is viable. Imagine planning a trip for someone without knowing where they want to go, what they enjoy, or what they're hoping to escape from—it wouldn't make sense. Similarly, crafting your digital marketing strategy without a comprehensive understanding of your audience is like setting sail without a compass. Tools like Google Analytics, social media insights, and direct surveys and polls provide a wealth of information about your audience, what they care about, and their challenges, enabling you to customize your content and offerings to align with their requirements.

The Intersection of Skills and Market Demand

Assessing how your skills meet the needs of your target audience involves a realistic appraisal of your strengths and how they align with market opportunities. Picture a musician skilled in an obscure instrument, finding an audience yearning for the unique sound it produces. Your 'instrument' in digital marketing could be anything from SEO wizardry to a knack for creating viral content. The key is identifying where your capabilities can address a market gap by offering value that draws your audience closer to your brand.

Lifestyle Alignment

Ensuring your chosen niche aligns with the lifestyle you aspire to is more than just work-life balance; it's about creating a harmonious existence where your professional endeavors and personal aspirations feed into each other positively. For instance, if travel and flexibility are cornerstones of the lifestyle you're aiming for, focusing on digital products or leveraging affiliate marketing might be more fitting than services requiring constant one-on-one interactions. This alignment enhances your happiness and lends credibility to your brand as you embody the values and lifestyle you promote.

Find Your Niche

This niche overview will cultivate questions to pinpoint the intersection between your passions, skills, and market needs. The overview narrows down potential niches that align with your personal and professional goals by answering questions about your interests, how you like to spend your time, and the type of people you enjoy helping. It's a practical tool that offers immediate insights, making the often complex task of niche selection a more manageable and enjoyable experience.

In navigating the journey for the perfect niche, remember that the goal is not to confine your creativity but to channel it where it will shine the brightest. It's about finding a segment of the digital world where your passion ignites the interest of an audience eagerly seeking what you have to offer. This journey of discovery is crucial since it lays the foundation upon which your digital marketing empire is built—one where your voice is heard, your brand is loved, and your business thrives.

2.2 RESEARCHING AND VALIDATING YOUR NICHE

Competitor Analysis

Navigating the terrain of your chosen niche necessitates a detailed exploration of those who have already claimed their spots in this domain. This exploration, known as competitor analysis, involves meticulously examining their strategies, strengths, weaknesses, and how they engage with their audience. Tools like SEMrush and Ahrefs offer insights into competitors' keyword strategies and backlink profiles, shedding light on their search engine visibility. Social media analysis further reveals how competitors connect with their audience, the content that resonates, and the opportunities in their strategies that you can leverage. This detailed scrutiny allows you to carve out a unique value proposition, positioning your brand not just as another option but as the preferred choice for your target audience.

Market Trends and Forecasts

A robust understanding of your niche's current landscape and future direction is crucial. This data is derived from quantitative data and qualitative insights, drawing from sources like Google Trends, industry reports, and thought leadership articles. Tools like BuzzSumo can reveal trending topics and content within your niche, offering a window into the interests and worries of your target audience. This exploration goes beyond just observation; it requires interpretation and analysis to predict how these trends will evolve and the implications for your niche. By staying ahead of the curve, you position yourself as a thought leader, guiding your audience through the changing landscape with confidence and authority.

Validation Techniques

Before fully committing your resources, validating your niche is a step that must be considered. This preliminary phase involves testing the waters with minimal investment, ensuring a receptive audience for your offering. Start by creating a minimal viable product (MVP) or service—a scaled-down version of your offering designed to gauge interest and gather feedback. Platforms like Kickstarter or Indiegogo can serve as testing grounds for product-based niches, while content creators might leverage social media or blogging platforms to measure engagement and interest. Collecting pre-orders or conducting small-scale ad campaigns with clear calls to action can provide tangible evidence of your niche's viability. This stage is less about profit and more about learning and refining your approach based on real-world data.

Feedback Loops

Constructing feedback loops with potential customers offers invaluable insights, turning abstract assumptions into concrete data. This iterative process begins with gathering initial reactions through surveys, social media interactions, or direct conversations. Tools like SurveyMonkey or Google Forms facilitate this process, allowing feedback collection that can inform adjustments to your offering. This feedback is not a one-time acquisition but part of an ongoing dialogue with your audience. Encourage reviews, engage in social media conversations, and invite comments on blog posts or forums. Analyzing this feedback requires a balance of objectivity and empathy, discerning the messages and underlying sentiments and needs. Based on this feedback, adjustments to your niche and offerings ensure that your direction aligns with your audience's desires and pain points. This process moves your niche toward greater resonance and relevance with your target market, solidifying your position and paving the way for sustained growth and engagement.

2.3 THE POWER OF MICRO-NICHES IN DIGITAL MARKETING

With the intricacy of digital marketing comes micro-niches. They represent the fine, often overlooked areas that, when properly evaluated, create their own unique categories. A micro-niche is a specialized segment within a broader market. It focuses on a specific interest group, offering tailored solutions that meet its unique needs and preferences. This hyper-focused approach facilitates a deeper connection with a targeted audience and significantly reduces competition, paving the way for enhanced visibility and profitability. Where broad markets are saturated with content and offers, micro-niches offer a sanctuary where genuine engagement and loyalty flourish.

The journey to uncover your micro-niche begins with a dissection of broader markets, peeling back layers to reveal the core interests and needs of smaller, highly passionate groups. This process involves leveraging data analytics to segment audiences based on their interactions, preferences, and behaviors. Social listening tools and keyword research also play critical roles, unveiling the topics and concerns that resonate most with these segments. Imagine a biologist under a microscope, each slide revealing more about the subject; similarly, each layer of data uncovers nuances about your potential micro-niche, guiding you toward an untapped or underserved market eager for your offerings.

Developing marketing strategies that resonate with your micro-niche requires an intimate understanding of the audience's language, pain points, aspirations, and the platforms they frequent. Specific content that addresses their interests, created with an authentic voice reflecting understanding and empathy, significantly increases engagement and conversion rates. For instance, leveraging micro-influencers within the niche who share a genuine enthusiasm for your offerings can amplify your message, causing a ripple effect that draws more attention to your brand. Additionally, personalized email marketing campaigns, utilizing segmentation and automation, ensure that your communications are relevant and timely, further cementing the relationship with your audience.

Exploring case studies of successful micro-niche strategies illuminates the path to crafting your own. Take, for instance, a small business that carved a niche in eco-friendly pet products. Focusing on pet owners passionate about sustainability, the company tailored its product development, content, and marketing efforts to address this group's specific concerns and preferences. The strategy included partnerships with eco-conscious influencers, participation in relevant online communities, and creating informative content around sustainability in pet care. This approach established the brand as a trusted authority in the niche and fostered a loyal customer base that identified strongly with the brand's values.

Another example is a digital marketer helping indie game developers market their games. By focusing on this narrow segment, the marketer could offer highly specialized services, from community building on platforms popular with gamers to crowdfunding campaigns that address the unique challenges faced by indie developers. These case studies exemplify how a deep dive into micro-niches and customized strategies can yield substantial rewards, positioning businesses as beloved brands within their communities.

Exploring micro-niches in digital marketing is not merely a strategy but a revelation of the power of specificity and personalization in building meaningful connections with your audience. It underscores the importance of genuinely understanding your audience and knowing their world, language, and needs. In a digital landscape cluttered with broad strokes and generic messages, the focus on micro-niches offers relevance and authenticity, attracting audiences looking for solutions that speak directly to them. The success stories woven from the threads of micro-niches serve as a testament to the potential in the meticulous crafting of marketing strategies that resonate personally, transforming passive observers into active, engaged communities. The deliberate and thoughtful integration of micro-niches is a testament to the enduring power of connection, relevance, and genuine engagement in forging paths to success and profitability.

2.4 CASE STUDIES: SUCCESSFUL NICHE MARKETING STRATEGIES

In a landscape where attention-grabbing is the main focus, niche marketing successes inspire and showcase invaluable wisdom. These narratives, each unique in their approach and outcomes, offer profound insights into the art of carving out distinct spaces within the digital expanse. Through exploring these case studies, we become aware of lessons on adaptability, innovation, and the strategic differentiation that propels niche brands to the forefront of their respective realms.

One such narrative unfolds with a small skincare brand that penetrated the oversaturated beauty market by catering exclusively to individuals with sensitive skin prone to allergies. This brand's journey began with a deep dive into forums and social media platforms where their target audience congregated, sharing their struggles and desires for products free from common irritants. Armed with this knowledge, the brand initiated a content marketing strategy emphasizing education about skincare ingredients, complemented by transparent product labeling. Their innovation lay in product formulation and creating an online community that served as a sanctuary for their audience, fostering loyalty and advocacy. This brand's trajectory highlights the potency of aligning product development and marketing strategies with a tight-knit community's specific needs and values, thereby achieving differentiation in a crowded market.

Another case study centers on an online platform dedicated to amateur bakers. Amidst the plethora of cooking websites and blogs, this platform distinguished itself by focusing on a niche that craved recipes and a deeper understanding of the science behind baking. The site's founders continuously adapted their content based on user feedback, incorporating interactive features such as Q&A sessions with professional bakers, user-generated recipe contests, and detailed guides on baking techniques. Their success was propelled by their commitment to creating a highly engaged online community where both novices and experienced bakers found value and camaraderie. This platform's growth illuminates the critical role that user engagement and community building play in elevating a niche brand beyond mere transactions to become a hub of shared passion and learning.

A startup carved its niche in eco-friendly products by focusing exclusively on sustainable outdoor gear. At the heart of their strategy was a commitment to transparency about the environmental impact of their products, from sourcing to production and disposal. They innovated by integrating a sustainability score on each product page, providing consumers with clear, actionable information to make environmentally conscious choices. This approach and a robust content marketing strategy highlighting sustainable outdoor practices positioned the brand as a trusted authority within the eco-conscious outdoor community. Their journey illustrates how a brand can differentiate itself through product offerings and embodying its target audience's values, fostering a deep, value-driven connection that transcends the traditional buyer-seller relationship.

A digital education company targeting aspiring digital marketers offers another valuable case study. Faced with intense competition, the company identified a micro-niche: digital marketers interested in leveraging artificial intelligence (AI) in their campaigns. By developing courses that delved into the practical applications of AI in digital marketing, the company met a specific, emerging need within the broader market. They further differentiated themselves by offering hands-on projects with real-world AI marketing tools, providing learners with theoretical knowledge and practical skills. This strategic focus on a micro-niche and an innovative approach to digital marketing education catapulted the company to a leading position within this specialized domain. Their success story demonstrates the power of micro-targeting and the importance of continually evolving content and offerings to align with the industry's cutting-edge trends and technologies.

Through these diverse narratives, several core lessons emerge. First, the capacity to adapt—whether to audience feedback, market trends, or technological advancements—emerges as a linchpin of success in niche marketing. Brands that remain agile, continuously refining their strategies and offerings in response to the evolving landscape, are those that thrive. Second, innovation, whether in product development, content creation, or community engagement, serves as a critical differentiator, setting niche brands apart in a sea of competitors. Lastly, the strategic differentiation of niche brands hinges on what they offer and how they connect with their audience, embodying their communities' values, interests, and aspirations. These case studies encapsulate the value in the larger picture of niche marketing success and offer insights for those willing to look beyond the surface to the strategic underpinnings that drive lasting impact and growth in the digital space.

2.5 AVOIDING COMMON NICHE SELECTION MISTAKES

Navigating the maze of niche selection in digital marketing demands a balance. Straying too far in either direction—toward a niche that's either excessively broad or unduly narrow—can come with its challenges, diluting marketing efforts or stifling potential growth. This approach often results in a diluted message that fails to resonate deeply with anyone. Conversely, honing in on a niche with laser precision might limit your audience size to the point where scalability becomes a concern. Finding the balance between these requires deep analysis, evaluating the market size, audience engagement levels, and the long-term viability of the niche. It's a process of calibration, where adjustments are made iteratively, ensuring the chosen niche is sufficiently focused to foster deep connections while offering ample room for growth.

Observing market data and emerging trends in the niche selection process is equivalent to navigating new walking grounds. Market data—from search trends to consumer behavior analytics—guides decisions in this digital reality. Ignoring or failing to integrate this data into strategic planning can lead to misaligned efforts that miss the mark in engaging the target audience. Moreover, trends offer a glimpse into the future direction of consumer interests, allowing for anticipatory adjustments in strategy. Incorporating this data requires a commitment to ongoing learning and adaptation, ensuring your marketing strategies evolve with the market's pulse.

An inherent flexibility in response to feedback and market shifts is required for sustained success in niche marketing. The reluctance to pivot, rooted in attachment to an initial vision or the inertia of existing strategies, can stifle innovation and hinder growth. Market landscapes are perpetually in flux, influenced by technological advancements, cultural shifts, and evolving consumer preferences. A niche that once seemed promising might wane in relevance, requiring a strategic pivot to remain aligned with market dynamics. Embracing this fluidity, viewing feedback as a valuable resource for refinement rather than criticism enables a dynamic approach to niche marketing. It's a stance that prioritizes resilience and responsiveness, qualities essential in the fast-paced digital arena.

Only underestimating the significance of consistent, high-quality content in establishing a foothold within your niche is a misstep with far-reaching implications. Content is the medium through which value is communicated, trust is built, and authority within the niche is established. Skimping content quality or consistency diminishes your brand's voice and erodes the audience's trust, a currency of immense value in the digital marketplace. Creating content that resonates, educates, and engages demands time and resources, underscoring the brand's commitment to its audience. This commitment fosters a loyal community, laying the groundwork for sustainable growth and positioning the brand as a beacon of expertise in its niche.

These pitfalls are a cautious reminder of the intricacy of niche selection and development, focusing the path toward a more informed and strategic approach. By navigating these challenges with foresight and adaptability, the potential of niche marketing is unlocked, paving the way for a brand to survive and thrive in the digital ecosystem.

Ultimately, niche selection is not about avoiding pitfalls; it's about being clear on a resonant narrative and creating a space where your brand can flourish. It's about recognizing the dynamic interplay between market needs, audience desires, and the unique value you offer. As we transition from the foundations laid in understanding and selecting a niche, our focus shifts toward the strategies that breathe life into these choices. The journey ahead is about activation—translating the insights into actionable strategies that captivate and convert.

CHAPTER 3
SCULPTING YOUR DIGITAL PERSONA

I magine a world where each of us has a monitor on us encapsulating the stories we've lived through. In this form of marketing, this monitor becomes your personal brand, a unique window that showcases who you are, what you stand for, and the journey that has shaped you. Your brand story isn't just a narrative; it's your most viable tool in connecting with your audience on a level that transcends the traditional. It's the heartbeat of your digital persona, pulsating through every tweet, post, and video, inviting your audience to step closer, to listen, and, most importantly, to trust.

3.1 CRAFTING YOUR PERSONAL BRAND STORY

Narrative is Key

A compelling brand story is akin to a magnet, drawing people in with its authenticity and resonance. Think of your favorite coffee shop, the one you repeatedly go to. Is it the quality of the coffee, the ambiance, or perhaps the story of the owner who left a corporate job to pursue a passion for artisanal coffee? That story adds a connection layer, transforming a simple coffee purchase into a personal and meaningful choice.

Crafting a narrative for your brand requires introspection and a willingness to share your triumphs, struggles, and lessons learned. It's about weaving the threads of your unique experiences into a story that not only defines your brand but also echoes the values and aspirations of your audience. This doesn't mean sharing every detail; it's about highlighting the moments that shaped your ethos, your approach, and, ultimately, your offerings.

Authenticity Sells

In an era where consumers are flooded with content, authenticity isn't just valuable; it's currency. It's the difference between a brand that feels like a friend and one that's just another advertiser vying for attention. Authentic storytelling fosters trust and loyalty, creating a basis for establishing a long-term connection with your audience. But authenticity can't be faked. It requires vulnerability, a readiness to share your true self, and the conviction to stand by your values, even when they go against the grain.

Connecting on a Personal Level

The power of personal connection in brand storytelling cannot be overstated. It's what transforms your narrative from a monologue into a dialogue, inviting your audience to see themselves in your story. Techniques for fostering this connection include:

- Sharing behind-the-scenes peeks into your process.
- Discuss the challenges you face and how you overcome them.
- Explaining the 'why' behind your work.

It's about finding the common threads that bind your story to your audience's experiences, hopes, and fears, making your brand seen and felt.

Imagine you're at a networking event, exchanging stories with someone you've just met. The conversation shifts from polite small talk to a shared story of a challenge overcome, a dream pursued, or a lesson learned the hard way. This shift forged a connection that will likely be remembered long after the event. Your digital brand story aims to replicate this moment of connection, bridging the gap between the screen and the heart.

Consistency Across Platforms

In the same way, a novel carries its thread through each chapter, your brand story must blend seamlessly across every platform you use. Consistency here is twofold: ensuring that your narrative remains coherent, whether someone encounters your brand on Instagram, LinkedIn, or your website. But it's also about ensuring that your story's tone, style, and essence adapt to fit each platform's unique language and culture while maintaining its core message. This consistency reinforces your brand identity, ensuring it is readily identifiable and trustworthy to your audience.

Crafting Your Brand Story

Explore your brand's core with unique pinpoints designed to uncover the narrative at the heart of your digital persona. This invites you to explore the pivotal moments, values, and passions that shape your story. Questions like "What moment in your life felt like a turning point in your career?" or "How do your values align with your professional goals?" serve as reflections and stepping stones in sculpting a brand story that is authentically yours.

In sculpting your digital persona, your brand story stands as the cornerstone, encapsulating what you offer and who you are. It's a narrative that requires honesty, introspection, and a willingness to share the journey that has shaped you. But beyond that, it's about forging a connection that transforms the digital space between you and your audience into a bridge built on trust, shared values, and the promise of a story worth following. Through this narrative, your brand becomes not just seen or heard but truly known.

3.2 SOCIAL MEDIA AS YOUR BRANDING PLAYGROUND

Social media emerges not merely as a tool for connection but as a dynamic canvas for branding, offering a spectrum of platforms, each with its unique culture, audience, and potential. Selecting the appropriate platforms is akin to choosing the suitable soil for the seeds you wish to sow; it requires understanding the terrain, climate, and what you intend to cultivate. This decision hinges on where your target audience allocates their attention and where your brand's essence can thrive. For example, a brand with a visually compelling story might find its home on Instagram or Pinterest. In contrast, a brand that thrives on real-time engagement and topical content might gravitate towards Twitter. This strategic selection ensures that your efforts are concentrated where they will flourish, allowing your brand to grow and resonate deeply with those you aim to reach.

Constructing a content strategy that reinforces your brand narrative while engaging your audience requires you to understand your chosen platforms. It's about curating content that speaks your truth and sparks conversations and connections. Through insightful blog posts shared on LinkedIn, captivating images on Instagram, or engaging discussions on Facebook, each piece of content should serve as a thread that incorporates your brand story into the fabric of your audience's daily lives. It's a detailed balance, maintaining the integrity of your message while adapting its expression to suit the medium and the listeners. Engaging content mirrors the audience's interests, challenges, and desires, effectively turning your social media pages into a reflection of your brand's essence and audience's aspirations.

Leveraging multimedia in your social media branding strategy introduces a layer of richness and depth, transforming static interactions into immersive experiences. Videos, images, and live streams act as windows, offering glimpses into the heart of your brand, the people behind it, and the values it embodies. A beautifully crafted video tells a story that words alone might not capture, conveying emotion and nuance in a manner that's instantly accessible and deeply impactful. On the other hand, live streams break down barriers, inviting your audience into real-time conversations and making them feel a part of your brand's journey. This multimedia approach diversifies your content and amplifies your brand's voice, allowing it to echo across the digital space visually and emotionally compellingly.

Fostering a community around your brand transforms your social media platforms from mere broadcasting channels into natural groups teeming with interaction, loyalty, and advocacy. This community building begins with active engagement - responding to comments, participating in relevant conversations, and creating content that invites interaction. However, it goes beyond mere responsiveness; it's about initiating dialogues, posing questions, and sparking debates that animate your community, making each member feel seen, heard, and valued. Hosting Q&A sessions, for instance, is not just about answering queries; it's an opportunity to delve into the concerns and curiosities of your audience, providing insights while learning about them. This engagement is a two-way street, a constant exchange that breathes life into your community, nurturing a sense of belonging among its members. It's about transforming followers into fans and customers into advocates by making them feel an essential part of your brand's narrative.

In the grand scheme, your social media platforms become not just stages for broadcasting your brand story but playgrounds where your audience can experience, interact with, and contribute to the narrative. It's a dynamic, ever-evolving landscape where your brand lives, breathes, and grows in the hearts and minds of those you reach. Through strategic platform selection, a robust content strategy, the creative use of multimedia, and genuine community engagement, your social media presence reflects your brand's essence, a beacon for those you seek to serve, and a testament to the connections you've nurtured. In this era, your brand's story is not just told; it's shared, experienced, and cherished, turning every post, tweet, and re-share into a thread in the larger tapestry of your brand's legacy.

3.3 VISUAL BRANDING: MORE THAN JUST A LOGO

Visual identity transcends basic aesthetics, shifting into a silent yet potent communicator of your brand's ethos, values, and story. This identity, encompassing logos, color schemes, typography, and imagery, serves as the visual handshake between your brand and the audience, setting the tone for the relationship afterward. Crafting this visual identity demands a strategic blend of design elements that resonate with your brand's core while appealing to the sensibilities of your target audience. It's akin to an artist selecting a palette before the brush even meets the canvas, where each color and stroke is deliberated to ensure the final piece embodies the intended message and emotion.

Creating a comprehensive visual identity system extends far beyond the confines of a logo. It's a detailed web of visual elements that coalesce to narrate your brand's story without saying a single word. Color schemes evoke emotions and communicate values at a glance. Typography conveys personality and tone, while imagery and graphics paint a vivid picture of your brand's world. This system acts as the visual vocabulary of your brand, enabling consistent and coherent communication across all touchpoints. It ensures that whether customers encounter your brand on social media, your website, or a billboard, they receive the same visual cues, reinforcing brand recognition and recall.

Harnessing visual branding to forge emotional connections with your audience is akin to composing a melody that resonates in the heart long after the music stops. Colors, for instance, wield the power to evoke a spectrum of emotions and associations, from the tranquility of blue to the energy of red. Typography, too, plays a pivotal role, with elegant serifs speaking to tradition and stability, while sleek sans-serifs echo modernity and innovation. The imagery further deepens this connection, with authentic, relatable visuals drawing the audience into your brand's narrative, making them feel part of your story. This emotional engagement is the linchpin in transforming passive viewers into passionate advocates, fostering a sense of belonging and loyalty that can't be compared to.

In such a place where change is the only constant, maintaining visual consistency across all marketing materials and online platforms is a challenge that demands meticulous attention. This consistency is the thread that navigates through the many touchpoints of your brand, creating a tapestry that is instantly recognizable. It's about ensuring that your website, social media profiles, email campaigns, and all other platforms speak in the same visual language, creating a smooth experience for your audience. This does not mean stifling creativity or variety but instead aligning all visual expressions with the core elements of your visual identity. It's a balancing act where creativity flourishes within the bounds of consistency, ensuring that your brand's visual identity remains cohesive, no matter where it appears.

The evolution of your brand requires periodic refreshes of your visual branding to ensure it remains relevant and resonant with your audience. This refreshing process is like shedding old skin, rejuvenating your brand, reflecting growth and adaptation to the changing world. However, this change must be approached with care, ensuring that the essence of your brand—the core elements that your audience has grown to know and trust—remains intact. It's about striking a balance between innovation and familiarity, ensuring that while the visual identity evolves, it still feels like the brand your audience has come to love. This could mean updating your color palette to reflect a more modern aesthetic, refining your logo to align with current trends, or revisiting your typography and imagery to better communicate your evolving brand story. The key is to involve your audience in this process, gathering their input and easing them into the transition, ensuring that the refresh strengthens their connection to your brand rather than alienating them.

In navigating the detailed process of crafting, maintaining, and refreshing your visual branding, the focus must always remain on creating a visual identity that encapsulates your brand's core and resonates deeply with your audience. It's a continuous journey of exploration, adaptation, and communication, where visual elements act as the messengers of your brand's values, story, and personality. Through strategic design and thoughtful implementation, visual branding becomes a powerful tool in building recognition, fostering emotional connections, and nurturing a loyal community around your brand. A solid visual identity stands as your core, guiding your audience through the many options so they can become close to your brand.

3.4 ENGAGING YOUR AUDIENCE WITH AUTHENTICITY

Personas are often curated with detailed precision. The essence of genuine interaction becomes a rare commodity, highly sought after by audiences craving connections that transcend the superficial layers of the social media gloss. This craving for authenticity serves as the guiding light to brands and individuals alike, urging them to peel back the facade and reveal the rawness of their narrative, being genuine. Authentic communication, therefore, emerges as a strategy and as a fundamental principle guiding how brands converse with their community, fostering an atmosphere of trust that nurtures unwavering loyalty.

The mastery of authentic communication hinges on an unspoken pact between brand and audience, a mutual acknowledgment of truth as the foundation of their interaction. This pact is honored through transparency in messaging, where honesty prevails over the temptation to embellish. It's reflected in the willingness to engage in open dialogue, addressing not just the highs but also the lows, the challenges alongside the triumphs. This approach demystifies the brand, positioning it not as an untouchable entity but as a companion on the audience's journey, one that shares, understands, and grows alongside them. In these moments of shared vulnerability, a deep, lasting bond is formed, resilient to the ebbs and flows of market trends and consumer behaviors.

The strategy of sharing behind-the-scenes content acts as a bridge, narrowing the division between brand and audience by inviting the latter into the former's world. This invitation is not to a polished showroom but to the workshop, the drawing board, the places where ideas take flight and where they sometimes falter. It's a glimpse into the process, the people, and the passion driving the brand, transforming it from an abstract concept into a living, breathing entity. This transparency humanizes the brand and ignites the audience's imagination, allowing them to see themselves as part of the narrative, co-creators in a continually unfolding story. It's a powerful testament to the brand's confidence in its mission and respect for the audience's intelligence and curiosity.

Feedback and criticism present a challenge, testing the brand's commitment to authentic communication. In this arena, defensiveness and evasion are the adversaries of trust, eroding the foundation built on transparency and honesty. Instead, a brand that listens, acknowledges, and responds with grace and humility to criticism stands as a form of integrity. This approach does not aim to mitigate the fallout but to learn from it and see feedback as a core unit to provide insight into the audience's needs and perceptions. It's an opportunity for growth, a chance to refine and improve, demonstrating that the brand's commitment to its audience extends beyond words. In this exchange, authenticity is both the shield and the sword, protecting the brand's integrity while cutting through the noise to reveal its true character.

Incorporating storytelling into branding elevates authentic communication into an art form, transforming messages into narratives that resonate deeply with the audience. Storytelling transcends the transactional nature of marketing, including a tapestry of experiences, emotions, and values that envelop the audience, inviting them to observe and feel. These stories are not fabrications but reflections of reality, tales of triumph and tribulation that echo the audience's experiences. They mirror the audience's desires, fears, and aspirations, creating a resonance that vibrates through the very core of their being. Through storytelling, the brand's narrative becomes interlaced with the audience's, creating a profound and personal bond. It's a connection beyond loyalty to a product or service; it becomes a loyalty to a shared story, a mutual journey that permeates the brand with an irreplaceable place in the audience's heart.

Searching for authenticity, brands navigate a landscape where the line between genuine interaction and curated presentation often blurs. Yet, those who commit to authentic communication, sharing the unfiltered reality of their journey, handling feedback with grace, and directing their narrative through storytelling discover a path to deep, meaningful connections with their audience. This path has challenges, requiring a balance of vulnerability and confidence, openness and strategy. However, for those willing to walk it, the rewards are immeasurable, forging relationships built on trust, respect, and a shared commitment to authenticity. In the digital age, where authenticity is rare and revered, these relationships become the cornerstone of brand success and a legacy that resonates through time, untouched by the shifting sands of trends and market dynamics.

3.5 MONITORING AND ADAPTING YOUR BRAND PRESENCE

The vigilance with which one tends to their online reputation can often delineate thriving brands from those that merely survive. This digital guardianship, online reputation management, demands strategies that safeguard and polish your brand's image in the ever-expansive digital universe. The essence of this endeavor lies in crafting a narrative that reflects your brand's core values and resonates with the audience's perceptions. It's a delicate balance, akin to walking a tightrope where the slightest misstep can tilt the scales. Navigating this landscape requires proactive measures that become indispensable, ranging from setting up alerts for brand mentions to regularly assessing customer feedback across platforms. This ongoing monitoring acts as an early alert system, enabling swift responses to potential issues before they escalate, ensuring that the narrative surrounding your brand remains positive and controlled.

Adapting to audience needs is an art form that requires an empathetic understanding of the shifting mind of consumer desires and expectations. In this dynamic interplay, feedback becomes the compass that guides the evolution of your brand messaging and content. It involves a keen ear tuned to the words spoken and the underlying currents of sentiment that flow through your audience's interactions with your brand. This adaptation is not reactionary but strategic, a calculated response that aligns your brand's evolution with the audience's evolving landscape.

It's a dance where the steps change to match the audience's needs, ensuring your brand remains relevant, engaging, and in tune with the times.

Staying relevant in the rapidly changing digital marketing ecosystem is the equivalent of charting a course through uncharted waters, where the only constant is change itself. This relevance is not merely about keeping pace with trends but about discerning which trends align with your brand's identity and which are fleeting distractions. It requires a discerning eye that can sift through the noise to find the signals that matter. Adjusting your branding strategy in response to these trends involves a blend of innovation and authenticity, ensuring that while your brand remains at the forefront of the industry, it retains its essence. Staying informed through industry reports, thought leadership, and competitor analysis becomes not just a task but a necessity, fueling the strategic pivots that keep your brand vibrant and visible in the crowded digital landscape.

In this endeavor, tools and software for brand monitoring emerge as invaluable allies, extending your reach and enhancing your insight into how your brand is perceived across the digital domain. These tools, sophisticated in their analytics yet intuitive use, offer a panoramic view of your brand's online presence. From social listening tools that capture the pulse of audience sentiment to analytics platforms that track engagement metrics, these resources provide a wealth of data that becomes the foundation for informed decision-making. They enable a refined analysis of interactions, highlighting areas of strength to be amplified and pinpointing weaknesses to be addressed. This stack of tools streamlines the process of brand monitoring and transforms data into actionable insights, driving the continuous refinement and enhancement of your brand's digital footprint.

As one navigates the building, maintaining, and evolving of a brand, the importance of monitoring and adapting your brand presence becomes abundantly clear. It's a process that demands vigilance, empathy, and strategic insight, ensuring that your brand resonates with your audience and remains a beacon of relevance in the ever-changing space. Through online reputation management, we safeguard our brand's narrative. Through adaptation, we ensure our messaging evolves with our audience's needs, and through staying informed, we keep our brand at the industry's forefront. Utilizing tools for brand monitoring, we transform data into insights, guiding our strategies and actions. This chapter underscores the dynamic nature of brand management in the digital realm, highlighting the need for continuous engagement, adaptation, and innovation. As we progress, we carry forward these themes, diving deeper into the strategies and tactics that enable brands to navigate and thrive in the digital marketing ecosystem.

CHAPTER 4
THE PILLARS OF VISIBILITY IN THE DIGITAL AGE

Standing at the threshold of digital visibility, one can't help but observe the activity of the online marketplace, where brands compete for attention amongst the array of options of the digital expanse. It's a place where the rules of engagement are dictated not by the loudest voice but by the most relevant; not by the flashiest advertisement, but by the most informative content. In this arena, the craftsmanship of Search Engine Optimization (SEO) emerges as a tactic and an essential lifeline, a guiding light through the thick plains of information overload.

Navigating this complex landscape requires more than intuition; it demands a deep understanding of the foundational pillars upon which digital marketing structure stands. It's like planting a garden in fertile land: understanding the soil (search engine algorithms), ensuring ample sunlight (mobile optimization), watering appropriately (integrating SEO with content marketing), and avoiding pests (steering clear of common SEO pitfalls) becomes critical for the garden to flourish.

4.1 SEO 101: UNDERSTANDING THE BASICS

Search Engine Algorithms

The enigma of search engine algorithms lies at the heart of SEO, a puzzle continuously evolving, each piece critical in determining how content is discovered and ranked. These algorithms have been created to mimic human behavior, sifting through vast information to present the user with the most relevant, helpful, and authoritative content. Understanding this, the first step towards optimizing content involves a meticulous analysis of keywords and phrases your audience uses to search for information. This is not about stuffing content with an arbitrary collection of words but about navigating these keywords naturally into valuable content that answers questions, solves problems, and enlightens the reader.

Importance of Mobile Optimization

Where the smartphone has become the window to the world for many, ensuring your website is mobile-friendly is no longer optional. It's a mandate dictated by user preference and search engine algorithms, with Google's mobile-first indexing serving as a testament to this shift. A mobile-optimized site is sleek, responsive, and accessible, offering a seamless user experience that keeps the audience engaged and reduces bounce rates. Picture going into a store where the aisles are cluttered and products are out of reach; the frustration that develops is comparable to navigating a non-mobile-friendly website on your smartphone.

SEO and Content Marketing Integration

The symbiosis between SEO and content marketing is like the relationship between rhythm and melody in a song; one cannot exist without the other. Content marketing provides the substance, the message, and the value, while SEO ensures that this message reaches the ears of those most eager to hear it. Integrating these two involves a strategic approach where content is crafted with the audience's needs in mind and with an understanding of how to make this content discoverable through SEO. It's about crafting content that will engage and resonate, then leveraging SEO, ensuring it ranks well to capture the audience's attention when they seek information.

Avoiding Common SEO Pitfalls

The path to SEO mastery is strewn with potential missteps, each capable of derailing your efforts and diminishing your visibility. Perhaps the most egregious of these is the temptation to engage in 'black hat' SEO tactics—practices that attempt to alternate search engine rankings through dishonesty. Not only do these tactics risk penalization by search engines, but they also erode trust with your audience. Another pitfall lies in neglecting the user experience, prioritizing search engines over the human beings interacting with your content. A site that is difficult to navigate, slow to load, or empty of valuable content may climb the rankings temporarily but ultimately fail to engage or convert visitors into loyal followers or customers.

SEO Essentials Checklist

A practical, actionable checklist designed to guide your initial foray into the world of SEO, ensuring every critical step is noticed. This checklist covers:

- Keyword research and integration
- Mobile optimization strategies
- Tips for integrating SEO with content marketing
- Common SEO pitfalls to avoid

This tool is a companion in your journey toward SEO proficiency. It offers a clear, step-by-step guide to crafting a strategy that enhances visibility, engages your audience, and lays the foundation for sustained digital growth.

4.2 MEASURING SEO SUCCESS WITH ANALYTICS

The efficacy of an SEO strategy is not gauged by the elegance of its execution nor the depth of its design but by tangible outcomes measured through the lens of analytics. This rigorous approach to evaluation transforms subjective assessments into objective data, offering a clear-eyed view of performance and paving the way for strategic refinement. Therefore, Setting SEO goals emerges as the initial step in this analytical journey, a process that demands precision in defining success. These goals, rooted in the SMART framework, encompass a spectrum from enhancing domain authority to elevating page rankings and boosting organic traffic. Each goal acts as a beacon, guiding the optimization efforts and providing a metric against which progress can be measured.

The website traffic analysis offers insights into visitors' behavior, shedding light on their paths, the content that captivates their interest, and the points at which they disengage. This scrutiny reveals not just the volume of traffic but its quality, distinguishing between fleeting visits and meaningful interactions. Tools like Google Analytics play a pivotal role in this endeavor, offering a granular view of user behavior, from the duration of visits to the bounce rates and conversion paths. Interpreting this data becomes an exercise in pattern recognition, identifying trends that signal success or highlight areas needing improvement. Within this analysis, the impact of SEO efforts is fully realized, offering a roadmap for enhancing user engagement and optimizing the website to serve the needs of its visitors better.

Tracking the performance of keywords stands at the core of SEO analytics. This practice transcends mere ranking assessment to dive into the efficacy of keywords in driving traffic and conversions. This involves monitoring the visibility of keywords in search results, their ability to attract clicks, and their contribution to achieving the set SEO goals. Adjusting the SEO strategy based on keyword performance becomes a dynamic process that requires agility in response to shifting search trends and competitive pressures. Tools specialized in keyword tracking offer insights into keyword rankings over time, providing a comparative analysis highlighting opportunities for strategic adjustments. This continuous cycle of monitoring, analyzing, and refining ensures that the SEO strategy remains aligned with the evolving landscape of search behavior and competitive dynamics.

Competitive analysis in the domain of SEO offers a window into the strategies employed by rivals, serving as a barometer against which to benchmark your performance. This analysis extends beyond a cursory review of competitors' rankings to a comprehensive assessment of their content strategy, backlink profile, and user engagement metrics. It unveils the strategies that underpin their SEO success and highlights gaps in their approach that present opportunities for differentiation. Engaging in this competitive analysis demands a strategic perspective that seeks not to emulate but to outmaneuver, identifying strengths to be leveraged and weaknesses to be ridden. Tools designed for competitive SEO analysis facilitate this exploration, offering insights into competitors' keyword strategies, the sources of their backlinks, and the architecture of their site optimization. Armed with this knowledge, refining your SEO strategy becomes a calculated endeavor, informed by data and driven by the objective to compete and excel in the crowded digital marketplace.

Measuring SEO success through analytics is an exercise in precision, a systematic approach to evaluating performance, understanding user behavior, and benchmarking against competitors. It transforms the nebulous realm of search optimization into a quantifiable field, where data and strategies guide decisions and are continually honed to align with the shifting dynamics of search and competition. Through this rigorous analytical lens, the path to SEO success becomes visible and navigable, marked by milestones of achievement and opportunities for strategic advancement.

4.3 ON-PAGE AND OFF-PAGE SEO TECHNIQUES

Optimizing Web Pages

The canvas of on-page SEO presents many opportunities for enhancing web pages' visibility and usability. The optimization of meta descriptions, those brief previews that appear beneath URLs in search results, stands as a critical endeavor. When artfully crafted, these snippets serve not as summaries alone but as compelling invitations, enticing users to click through to your website. Equally vital are header tags, the signposts that guide readers through the labyrinth of content, making it digestible and enhancing its appeal to search engines. They delineate structure, emphasizing key points and ensuring that content isn't just a block of text but a landscaped garden of information. Furthermore, including image alt text transcends accessibility, offering search engines a textual descriptor of visuals, thereby adding images to the SEO space. Each element, from meta descriptions to header tags and image alt text, contributes to the tapestry of on-page SEO, enhancing user experience and rankings.

Building Backlinks

In the realm of off-page SEO, the construction of backlinks emerges as a cornerstone, a testament to a website's authority and relevance. When anchored on external sites, these links act as bridges, guiding traffic and credibility back to your digital doorstep. The strategies for building these connections range from guest blogging on esteemed platforms to engaging in influencer collaborations and creating shareable, high-quality content that naturally garners links. Each backlink acquired serves as an endorsement in the view of search engines, elevating your site's standing and visibility. However, this pursuit demands discernment, focusing on the quality of links rather than mere quantity, ensuring that each backlink is a sturdy bridge rather than a fragile thread.

Local SEO Optimization

The essence of local SEO lies in its ability to connect businesses with the community around them, transforming the internet's global reach into a localized handshake. This optimization involves tailoring your website's content to include local keywords, ensuring that your business appears in local search results, and enhancing your presence on platforms like Google My Business. The meticulous inclusion of local details, from address and phone number to local landmarks and events, weaves your business into the local narrative, making it visible and accessible to those nearby. This localized focus transforms search engines from vast oceans to neighborhood streams, directing local traffic directly to your door.

Monitoring Your SEO Performance

The vigilance in monitoring SEO performance unfolds as a relentless journey, a continuous loop of measurement, analysis, and adjustment. Tools designed for this purpose offer a panoramic view of a website's SEO health, tracking everything from keyword rankings and backlink quality to page loading speed and mobile responsiveness. This arsenal of data serves not as an endpoint but as a starting point for strategic adjustments, pinpointing areas of strength to be bolstered and weaknesses to be remedied. The dynamic nature of SEO demands this constant vigilance, ensuring that your digital presence remains visible and vibrant in the ever-shifting landscape of search engine algorithms.

In this tug-of-war of on-page and off-page SEO techniques, the art lies not in the execution of isolated tactics but in their orchestration, each move informed by data and driven by the goal of enhancing visibility and engagement. Through the meticulous optimization of web pages, the strategic building of backlinks, the localized focus of SEO efforts, and the relentless monitoring of performance, the path to SEO mastery becomes navigable and navigated, marked by the milestones of increased visibility, engagement, and conversion.

4.4 SETTING UP A WEBSITE THAT SELLS

In this marketplace, where countless businesses fight for attention, a website emerges as a core foundation where visitors are transformed into patrons. This metamorphosis is underpinned by aesthetic allure and navigational ease, a domain where user experience (UX) design reigns supreme. In its essence, UX design is the alchemy of crafting digital spaces that are intuitively navigable, visually harmonious, and conducive to the seamless journey of the visitor from curiosity to conversion. It transcends the superficial layer of design, delving into the visitor's psyche, anticipating needs, and eradicating barriers to engagement. This realm is where colors, fonts, and layouts are not arbitrary choices but deliberate strategies, each contributing to a cohesive experience that beckons the visitor deeper into the brand narrative, culminating in the ultimate act of commitment: conversion.

Parallel to the architectural elegance of UX design, the content strategy for your website acts as the lifeblood, nourishing visitor engagement with a steady stream of valuable, relevant, and compelling narratives. This strategy requires deep diving into the brand ethos, clearly understanding the audience's desires and challenges, and crafting content that bridges the two. It's an endeavor that goes beyond keyword stuffing, aiming instead to provide answers, inspire thought, and evoke emotion, thereby positioning your brand not as a vendor but as a thought leader and a trusted advisor in the visitor's search for solutions. The art of content strategy lies in its ability to weave a narrative thread through every page and post, creating a tapestry of captivating and informative information, driving engagement, and fostering loyalty.

The foundation upon which this digital building stands is the choice of a domain and hosting service, decisions that, while seemingly logistical, are fraught with implications for scalability, security, and search engine visibility. Selecting a domain name would be the equivalent of choosing a title for a book; it must be memorable, relevant, and reflective of the brand's essence, serving as a monument in the vast sea of the internet, guiding visitors to your digital shore. On the other hand, the choice of hosting service is about ensuring that this beacon remains luminous, even in the face of surging traffic and potential security threats. It's about finding a partner capable of supporting your website's growth, ensuring uptime, and safeguarding data, thereby providing a stable and secure platform upon which the brand can build its digital presence.

Amidst this intricate web of design, content, and logistics, website analytics emerge as the compass, guiding strategic decisions and illuminating the path to enhanced user engagement and increased conversion rates. Implementing analytics is not an exercise in data collection but an ongoing strategy of listening to the digital footprints left by visitors. It offers a window into the visitor's journey through your website, from the pages that captivate their attention to the ones that trigger departure, providing actionable insights that drive continuous improvement. Analytics enable the fine-tuning of UX design, the refinement of content strategy, and the optimization of overall website performance. It's a process of consistent evolution, where data informs decisions, decisions shape experiences, and experiences culminate in the website's ability to attract visitors and convert them into loyal customers.

In a space where attention can be fleeting, creating a website that sells is an endeavor of both art and science. It requires a harmonious blend of UX design principles, a strategic content approach, informed choices in domain and hosting, and a commitment to analytics-driven improvement. This fusion elevates the website from a digital entity to a dynamic marketplace. It is evidence of the brand's commitment to delivering value, enhancing user experience, and fostering engagement. In this digital age, a website that sells is not merely a platform for transactions but a crucible where visitor interactions are converted into lasting relationships, setting the stage for sustained business growth and success.

4.5 KEYWORD RESEARCH AND CONTENT CREATION

Uncovering the most resonant keywords in these algorithms that govern the digital realm is a detailed process. This process, rooted in science and intuition, demands a thorough exploration of the language and queries your audience employs in their search for answers. This exploration transcends guesswork, leveraging tools designed to mine the depths of search data, revealing the words and the intent behind them. It's an endeavor that mirrors the work of an archaeologist, sifting through layers to uncover relics that tell the story of human curiosity and need. The selection of these keywords, therefore, becomes a strategic endeavor, balancing volume with relevance, ensuring that each term selected serves as a beacon, guiding your audience through the digital noise to the sanctuary of your content.

Crafting content that connects users and search engines is similar to composing a symphony, where each note must harmonize with the next, crafting a piece that delights the audience while adhering to rigorous performance standards. This creation process involves a delicate balance, embedding keywords within valuable, informative, and compelling narratives that capture the audience's attention and keep them engaged. The principles guiding this craftsmanship emphasize not just the strategic placement of keywords but the flow of information, the structure of the narrative, and the quality of the insights provided. It's a blend of artistry and precision, where each piece of content serves a primary purpose: to enlighten the reader and to indicate to search engines the authority and relevance of the information presented.

Using long-tail keywords introduces specificity and intent to the content strategy, targeting queries that, while less frequent, are imbued with a higher potential for conversion. These phrases, often more conversational and detailed, reflect the natural language patterns of users, especially in the age of voice search. By focusing on these long-tail keywords, content is created to add traffic and attract the right traffic, individuals on the cusp of decision-making, seeking detailed, nuanced answers that your content provides. This approach transforms content from a broad net into a precision instrument, honed to capture the attention of those most likely to engage deeply with your brand.

Developing a content calendar that seamlessly integrates these keywords into a cohesive, strategic narrative represents the peak of this endeavor. This calendar acts as a schedule and a strategic blueprint outlining the topics, formats, and keywords that will guide content creation over time. It ensures consistency, not just in the frequency of posts but in the quality and relevance of the content provided. This planning allows flexibility, responding to emerging trends and audience needs while maintaining a steady drumbeat of content that reinforces your brand's authority and relevance. It's a map that navigates the ebbs and flows of digital engagement, ensuring that at every turn, your content remains a beacon of value and insight, drawing your audience ever closer to your brand.

In the grand scheme, keyword research and content creation are pivotal threads, intertwining to form a strategy that attracts, engages, and converts. This process, marked by meticulous research, strategic creativity, and consistent execution, lays the groundwork for a digital presence that resonates with authority and relevance. Through carefully selecting keywords, crafting SEO-friendly content, strategically using long-tail keywords, and developing a content calendar, brands forge connections with their audience that transcend the transactional, nurturing relationships that are both meaningful and enduring.

As we wrap up this chapter, we recognize the intricate interplay between keyword research and content creation as fundamental to navigating the digital landscape. This journey, grounded in strategic insight and creative expression, sets the stage for the subsequent exploration of digital marketing's vast potential. The insights garnered here serve as a foundation for more advanced strategies and tactics, each step forward guided by relevance, engagement, and authenticity principles.

CHAPTER 5

NAVIGATING THE SOCIAL MEDIA LANDSCAPE

Social media platforms stand as lighthouses, guiding brands toward their desired audiences with precision and flair. These platforms are not solely communication channels; they are vibrant ecosystems teeming with life, each with its unique culture, language, and community. The art of choosing the right platform for your brand is like selecting the perfect habitat where your message will not only survive but thrive. It's about understanding the subtle nuances of each environment and aligning them with your brand's voice, goals, and audience demographics.

Navigating this field requires a map that goes beyond popularity or user count. It demands a deep dive into each platform's strengths and features, a deep understanding of your audience's online behavior, and a strategy that ensures brand consistency across all channels. This exploration is not a solitary endeavor but a collaborative journey with your audience, understanding their preferences, habits, and expectations to create a presence that resonates and engages.

5.1 CHOOSING THE RIGHT PLATFORMS FOR YOUR BRAND

Audience Demographics

An effective social media marketing tool is understanding how your audience spends time online and where exactly that is. It's like planning a party; you need to know where your guests like to hang out to choose the right venue. For instance, if your brand targets professionals and industry leaders, LinkedIn's environment, which focuses on career development and professional networking, might be where your message resonates the most. Conversely, suppose your audience skews younger and prefers visual content. In that case, platforms like Instagram and TikTok offer fertile ground for engagement through dynamic imagery and video content. Tools like Pew Research Center's social media fact sheets provide invaluable insights into the user demographics of various platforms, helping brands make informed decisions about where to establish their presence.

Platform Strengths

Every social media platform is unique, and it has strengths that can amplify your brand's message. For example, Twitter excels at real-time engagement and topical content, making it ideal for brands looking to participate in current conversations or offer quick customer service responses. With its emphasis on visual discovery, Pinterest is a power-house for brands in the lifestyle, decor, and fashion sectors, offering a visually rich medium to showcase their products. Recognizing and leveraging these strengths allow brands to customize their engagement and content strategies for the platform's specific characteristics, maximizing impact and reach.

Brand Consistency

While each platform offers unique opportunities for engagement, ensuring a consistent brand voice and aesthetic across all channels is crucial. This consistency acts as a thread that weaves through the various platforms, creating a cohesive brand identity that's easily recognizable. It's about ensuring that your brand feels familiar to your audience, whether scrolling through Instagram, tweeting on Twitter, or networking on LinkedIn. This doesn't mean posting identical content across all platforms but adapting your message to fit the platform's format and audience while maintaining your core brand identity.

Strategic Platform Selection

Deciding which platforms to focus on goes beyond current trends. It requires a forward-looking approach, anticipating where your audience might migrate next and which platforms are poised for growth. For instance, with its audio-based networking, emerging platforms like Clubhouse offer new avenues for brands to engage with audiences in a more personal and compelling format. Some other platforms that encompass the same avenues include Telegram and even Discord. Staying ahead of these trends and being open to experimenting with new platforms can position your brand as an innovator, capturing the attention of early adopters and setting the stage for future growth.

Find Your Perfect Social Media Match

These examples offer personalized, thought-provoking frameworks for selecting your brand's social media platforms. You will be guided toward the platforms where your brand will flourish by answering questions about your brand's primary goals, target audience demographics, preferred content format, and engagement style. This tool is practical for brands at any stage of their social media journey, providing insights and suggestions customized to their specific requirements and objectives.

Choosing the right social media platforms for your brand involves a strategic blend of understanding your audience, leveraging each platform's unique strengths, ensuring brand consistency, and staying attuned to emerging trends. It's a critical step in establishing a social media presence that connects with your target audience and engages them meaningfully, building connections beyond the digital aspect. As brands navigate this complex landscape, their choices in platform selection lay the groundwork for their social media success, shaping their interactions with current and future audiences.

5.2 CREATING ENGAGING AND SHARE-WORTHY CONTENT

Crafting content that captivates and compels the audience to engage and share is an endeavor that combines creativity with strategy. Narratives and visuals are woven into a fabric that blankets the audience with relevance and resonance. This multifaceted task requires an adept understanding of the elements that unite to form content that stands not merely seen or heard but felt and remembered, prompting action in the form of shares and interactions that amplify its reach.

Content Value

The cornerstone of engaging content lies in its inherent value to the audience, a combination of insights, entertainment, education, and inspiration that enriches the user experience. This value is multifaceted, encompassing the ability to answer pressing questions, solve persistent problems, or provide a much-needed respite from the mundanity or challenges of daily life. It's guiding the audience toward enlightenment, empowerment, or escape. Crafting such content demands an intimate acquaintance with the audience's desires, fears, and curiosities, transforming each piece of content into a key that unlocks a more profound understanding, skill, or perspective. This endeavor, rooted in empathy and bolstered by research, ensures that every article, video, and post serves as a bridge, connecting the brand's expertise and offerings with the audience's needs and aspirations.

Visual Appeal

In the visually saturated realm of social media, the pull of high-quality, visually appealing images and videos must be noticed. This pull is aesthetic and strategic, capturing attention in the fleeting moments as thumbs scroll screens, stopping users in their tracks and inviting them into your narrative. The power of a compelling image or an engaging video lies in its ability to convey complex messages, evoke emotions, and encapsulate stories in a format that's instantly accessible and universally understood. The selection and creation of such visuals require a keen eye for composition, color, and context, ensuring each visual element aligns with the brand's identity and message while resonating with the audience's aesthetic preferences and cultural nuances. This visual storytelling, when executed with precision and artistry, transforms content from static to dynamic, encouraging engagement and sharing as users are moved to extend the impact of the content through their networks.

Emotional Connection

The foundation of share-worthy content is created with the strands of emotional connection. This bond transcends the transactional and forges a unique relationship between the brand and the audience. This connection is cultivated through narratives that touch upon universal human experiences, evoke shared dreams, or stir common fears, drawing the audience closer with each word, image, or video. It's about recognizing the content as a medium for empathy, a channel for expressing and addressing the emotional undertones that color the audience's perceptions and experiences. Crafting content that achieves this level of connection demands an authentic voice that speaks from experience, from the heart, and from a place of a genuine desire to enrich the audience's life. This authenticity imbues content with the power to move, resonate, and be shared as audiences see their reflections in the stories told and are compelled to pass on the message.

Trending Topics

The ebb and flow of trending topics and hashtags dictate the pulse of social media. These currents carry with them the potential to elevate content visibility and engagement to new heights. Tapping into these trends is a strategic maneuver, aligning content with the conversations that captivate the audience's attention at any moment. However, this alignment is more than opportunism; it is finding the intersection where trending topics meet the brand's expertise and audience's interests. It's a balance, ensuring that the content not only gains the visibility afforded by the trend but also adds value to the conversation, offering insights, perspectives, or entertainment that enriches the discourse. This approach requires agility, the ability to quickly adapt content strategies to leverage trends while maintaining the integrity and relevance of the message. When mastered, this can propel content across the digital landscape, increasing the shares and interactions.

Crafting content that resonates, engages, and compels the audience to share is an art form, a symphony of value, visual appeal, emotional connection, and timely relevance. It's about understanding the audience deeply, speaking to their needs and desires, and presenting narratives and visuals that strike a chord, compelling them to extend the reach of the content through their networks. This endeavor, rooted in empathy, creativity, and strategic agility, transforms content from only information to an experience. This shared journey binds the audience to the brand in a relationship marked by trust, loyalty, and mutual enrichment.

5.3 SOCIAL MEDIA SCHEDULING AND AUTOMATION TOOLS

In the labyrinthine world of social media, where timing is as crucial as content quality, the strategic use of scheduling and automation tools emerges as an anchor for digital marketers aiming to optimize their online presence. Platforms such as Buffer, Hootsuite, or Later represent technological conveniences and strategic assets that stream-line content distribution, ensuring that postings' rhythm aligns perfectly with audience activity peaks. These tools, sophisticated in their algorithmic skill, enable the pre-planning of content dissemination, transforming the chaotic nature of real-time posting into a harmonized symphony that reaches the audience at moments of maximum receptivity.

The essence of maintaining a consistent posting schedule transcends mere frequency of updates; it's about estab-lishing a reliable presence that audiences can anticipate and rely upon. This consistency, facilitated by the tools mentioned above, guides your audiences through the noise of their crowded social feeds to the shores of your content. The predictability of your posting schedule fosters a sense of familiarity and expectation, crucial elements in culti-vating audience engagement and loyalty. It's like a favorite television show that airs at a set time, where viewers arrange their schedules to tune in, transforming passive consumption into an active, engaged ritual.

Leveraging tools equipped with analytics features offers a window into the performance of each post, turning raw data into actionable insights. These analytics capabilities allow for a granular examination of engagement metrics, reach, and conversion rates, providing a clear picture of content resonance and areas for optimization. Adjusting strategies based on this data becomes dynamic, where content, timing, and audience targeting are continually refined to enhance performance. It's a systematic approach, where each piece of data serves as a clue in unraveling the preferences and behaviors of the audience, enabling marketers to tailor their strategies with precision and agility.

The realm of engagement monitoring, facilitated by automation tools, ensures that the digital conversation between brand and audience remains vibrant and responsive. These tools offer real-time alerts on comments, mentions, and direct messages, enabling brands to sustain active interaction with their community without the constraints of constant manual monitoring. This responsiveness breeds a culture of attentiveness, signaling to the audience that their voices are heard and valued. It transforms the brand presence from a monologue into a dialogue, fostering a sense of community and connection that enhances brand loyalty. Engagement monitoring acts as the brand's ears and eyes on the digital ground, capturing the nuances of audience sentiment and feedback, informing content strategy and community management practices.

The strategic deployment of scheduling and automation tools is a testament to the fusion of technology and strategy. Optimizing with these tools, posting schedules, harnessing analytics for strategic refinement, and maintaining active engagement empowers brands to reach and strike a chord with their audiences meaningfully. They represent not just a means to an end but a transformative approach to social media marketing, where efficiency, consistency, and responsiveness converge to create a digital presence that is both vibrant and impactful. Through this lens, social media scheduling and automation tools are not merely technological aids but strategic companions in the journey toward digital marketing excellence, enabling brands to navigate confidently.

5.4 BUILDING AND NURTURING AN ONLINE COMMUNITY

Cultivating an online community transcends mere follower accumulation; it calls for a blend of strategies to foster meaningful interactions, a sense of belonging, and mutual growth. This endeavor, while intricate, is not impossible. It begins with a commitment to active engagement, ensuring that each comment, query, and message receives acknowledgment and a thoughtful response. This level of interaction signals to your followers that their voices are heard and valued, transforming passive observers into engaged participants in your brand's narrative.

The encouragement of user-generated content (UGC) is a powerful catalyst in community building, inviting followers to contribute their perspectives, experiences, and creativity. This approach enriches the content ecosystem with diverse viewpoints and instills a sense of ownership and pride among community members. It's like inviting guests into your home and encouraging them to decorate the walls with artwork, instilling a collective identity that resonates with warmth and inclusivity. Competitions, challenges, and themed content prompts can effectively stimulate user-generated content, weaving the individual threads of your community into a vibrant tapestry of shared experiences.

Creating exclusive groups or forums offers a place for deeper connection and engagement, a sanctuary where like-minded individuals can congregate, share insights, and support one another. Platforms such as Facebook Groups, Discord servers, or, more recently, Skool communities provide the infrastructure for these micro-communities, spaces where conversations can flourish away from the public eye, fostering a sense of intimacy and exclusivity. These groups become extensions of your brand and entities in their own right, characterized by the unique dynamics, culture, and relationships that evolve within. They offer a real-time feedback, originality, and collaboration platform, enabling you to tap into your community's collective wisdom and creativity, enhancing your offerings and strategies in alignment with their needs and preferences.

Providing consistent value through tips, insights, and insider information is pivotal in nurturing these communities. This continuous stream of value serves as the lifeblood of the community, keeping members engaged, informed, and motivated. It's about offering more than just products or services; it provides knowledge, inspiration, and solutions that enrich your audience's lives. Whether through educational webinars, exclusive behind-the-scenes content, or early access to new offers, the goal is to contribute positively to your community's knowledge base and experience, cementing your brand's position as a provider and as a mentor in their journey.

This nurturing process of community building—rooted in active engagement, the cultivation of user-generated content, the creation of exclusive groups, and the consistent delivery of value—requires a nuanced understanding of human dynamics, a genuine interest in fostering relationships, and a commitment to continuous improvement. It is an ongoing endeavor characterized by the ebb and flow of interactions, feedback, and growth. Through this process, brands have the opportunity to transcend the traditional boundaries of consumer relationships, forging communities that are not only loyal but also empowered, inspired, and connected.

5.5 ANALYZING SOCIAL MEDIA METRICS FOR BETTER ROI

In a space where data reigns supreme, the meticulous analysis of social media metrics becomes the crucible, and practical strategies are forged to accurately capture the return on investment (ROI). This pursuit clarifies what interactions and insights comprise your brand's digital presence. The selection of key performance indicators (KPIs) emerges as the initial step in this analysis. This deliberate action aligns the heartbeat of your social media endeavors with the broader aspirations of your business. These KPIs, from engagement rates to conversion ratios, guide your strategy, highlighting the path toward visibility and tangible success.

The groundwork for measuring these metrics spans from the native analytics tools embedded within each social media platform to sophisticated third-party instruments that offer a panoramic view of your digital footprint. Platforms like Facebook or Instagram Insights and Twitter Analytics provide a window into the soul of your campaigns, revealing the resonance of your content and your audience's demographics with startling clarity. Meanwhile, tools like Google Analytics and Sprout Social extend this vision, offering cross-platform comparisons and deeper dives into user behavior and campaign performance. This diverse toolkit equips you with the means to distill raw data into actionable intelligence, transforming the momentary interactions of likes, shares, and comments into a coherent narrative that allows for strategic decisions.

The refinement of your social media strategy, informed by this data, assumes the form of alchemy, where knowledge from past campaigns transmutes into the key to optimized future endeavors. This process demands an openness to adaptation, where strategies evolve in response to the shifting sands of audience behavior and platform algorithms. Each step is informed by insights into what captivates your audience, what drives engagement, and what converts interest into action-taking. This nuanced approach ensures that your social media efforts are not shots in the dark but targeted campaigns that strike the heart of your audience's desires, maximizing impact and ROI.

While complex, calculating ROI from your social media activities anchors these efforts in the tangible realm, offering a clear-eyed view of the value derived from each tweet, post, and share. This calculation, incorporating both the direct costs of your campaigns and the indirect expenses of time and labor, provides a holistic assessment of your social media investment. Employing formulas that compare this investment against the revenue generated - whether through direct sales, lead conversions, or enhanced brand visibility - unveils the true impact of your social media endeavors. This insight, invaluable in its clarity, guides not just budgetary allocations but strategic pivots, ensuring that your social media presence is vibrant and vitally contributory to your business's growth and success.

In the intricacy of social media marketing, the analysis of metrics and the calculation of ROI stand as a testament to the power of data-driven strategy. This approach, marrying the art of content creation with the science of analytics, transforms social media from a platform of expression into a conduit for growth. It underscores the importance of speaking to your audience and listening to the data about their preferences, behaviors, and responses. Through this lens, social media becomes a dynamic landscape where every interaction holds the potential for insight, every campaign a lesson in optimization, and every strategy a step toward achieving visibility and tangible, measurable success.

In the broader context of digital marketing, the meticulous analysis of social media metrics illuminates the path to understanding the impact of your efforts and optimizing them for greater efficiency and ROI. This chapter has unveiled the strategies and tools at your disposal, guiding you through the selection of KPIs, the utilization of analytics tools, the refinement of strategy, and the calculation of ROI, each step a deliberate move toward aligning your social media endeavors with your broader business goals. As we transition from the focused lens of social media to the expansive vista of digital marketing, these insights serve as the foundation for more advanced strategies and tactics, ensuring that every effort is informed, targeted, and poised for success.

MAKE A DIFFERENCE WITH YOUR REVIEW
UNLOCK THE POWER OF GENEROSITY

"Money can't buy happiness, but giving it away can."

FREDDIE MERCURY

People who give without expectation live longer, happier lives and make more money. So if we've got a shot at that during our time together, darn it, I'm gonna try.

To make that happen, I have a question for you…

Would you help someone you've never met, even if you never got credit for it?

Who is this person you ask? They are like you. Or, at least, like you used to be. Less experienced, wanting to make a difference, and needing help, but unsure where to look.

My mission is to make Digital Marketing knowledge accessible to everyone. Everything I do stems from that mission, and the only way for me to accomplish that mission is by reaching… everyone.

This is where you come in. Most people do, in fact, judge a book by its cover (and its reviews). So here's my ask on behalf of a struggling Digital Marketer you've never met:

Please help that online marketer by leaving this book a review.

Your gift costs no money and takes less than 60 seconds to make real, but it can change a fellow Digital Marketer's life forever. Your review could help…

- one more small business provide for their community.
- one more entrepreneur support their family.
- one more employee get meaningful work.
- one more client transform their life.
- one more dream come true.

To get that 'feel good' feeling and help this person for real, all you have to do is leave a review, and it takes less than 60 seconds.

Scan the QR code to leave your review:

If you feel good about helping a faceless Digital Marketer, you are my kind of person that I like and respect. Welcome to the club. You're one of us.

I'm even more excited to help you create your own successful Digital Marketing business faster and easier than you can possibly imagine. You'll love the lessons and strategies I'll share in the coming chapters.

Thank you from the bottom of my heart. Now, back to our regularly scheduled programming.

Your biggest supporter, Amelia Koonjbeharry

PS - Fun fact: If you provide something of value to another person, it makes you more valuable to them. If you'd like goodwill straight from another Online Marketer - and you believe this book will help them - send it their way.

CHAPTER 6

AMPLIFYING YOUR BRAND THROUGH SOCIAL MEDIA ADVERTISING

Social media platforms, the core of where your audience lies, are one of the most viable tools at your fingertips. Understanding how to make your brand transferable between various platforms is critical. The challenge lies in making sure your offer catches the eye of your audience based on the platform that they're on and knowing how to interact with them from that point. Social media advertising is the key to singling out your brand and what allows it to stand apart. This chapter explores the strategies and nuances of crafting social media ad campaigns that capture attention and convert curiosity into meaningful engagement and loyalty.

6.1 LAUNCHING SUCCESSFUL SOCIAL MEDIA AD CAMPAIGNS

Ad Platform Selection

The first critical step in launching an effective social media ad campaign is selecting the right platform. This decision mirrors the process of choosing the perfect fishing spot, where understanding the water, the fish, and the best bait makes all the difference. Each social media platform, with its unique user demographics and behavior patterns, offers distinct opportunities for reaching your target audience. For instance, LinkedIn's professional environment is ideal for B2B marketing, while Instagram's visually rich landscape caters well to brands with compelling visual content, whereas Facebook's marketplace offers broader audience targeting. This choice hinges on where your audience spends their time and how they interact with content, ensuring your ads are placed where they will naturally attract attention, engagement, and conversion.

Targeting and Segmentation

Once the platform is chosen, the focus shifts to targeting and segmentation, like selecting the right lure for the fish you aim to catch. Advanced targeting options on platforms like Facebook and Instagram allow marketers to refine their audience based on demographics, interests, behaviors, and more. This precision ensures your ads reach the individuals most likely to be interested in your offering, maximizing your ad spend and boosting conversion rate. It's about understanding the nuances of your audience, segmenting them into distinct groups, and tailoring your messaging to resonate with each segment's unique needs and preferences.

Creative Ad Content

Creating ad content that resonates with your target audience is just crafting a compelling story that captivates from the first word to the last. This content, whether an eye-catching image, an engaging video, or a thought-provoking text, serves as the hook that draws the audience in. It must speak directly to their desires, challenges, and aspirations, offering solutions, inspiration, or entertainment that aligns with their interests. The creative process involves an understanding of your audience and an ability to distill your brand's essence into content that is both memorable and compelling. It's about balancing creativity and clarity, ensuring your message is delivered effectively within the constraints of the ad format and platform specifications.

Campaign Analysis and Adjustment

The final piece in the puzzle is the continuous analysis and adjustment of your ad campaigns, a process that mirrors the refinement of a recipe based on feedback from those who taste it. Through the use of analytics tools provided by social media platforms, marketers can track the performance of their ads in real time, measuring engagement, reach, conversion rates, and more. This data provides invaluable insights into what works and what doesn't, allowing adjustments to optimize campaign performance. Whether tweaking the ad copy, adjusting the targeting parameters, or exploring different creative formats, this iterative process ensures your social media advertising efforts constantly evolve, improve, and move closer to achieving your marketing objectives.

Campaign Optimization

This serves as a guide, ensuring every aspect of your social media ad campaign is meticulously planned and executed. From selecting the right platform, targeting the appropriate audience segments, creating compelling ad content, and continuously analyzing performance, each item on the checklist is designed to optimize your campaign for maximum impact. Use this to evaluate your campaign's readiness, identify improvement areas, and enhance your strategy for better results.

Social media advertising offers a path to visibility, engagement, and conversion. Through strategic platform selection, precise targeting, creative content development, and continuous campaign analysis, brands can cut through the noise, capturing the attention of their target audience and fostering meaningful connections. This lays the groundwork for successful social media ad campaigns, combining strategic insight with practical tools and tips to empower marketers to amplify their brand's presence.

6.2 INFLUENCER COLLABORATIONS AND SPONSORSHIPS

Forging alliances with influencers is a nuanced strategy, blending the art of connection with the science of engagement. This alliance represents a confluence of visions and values, where the influencer's authentic voice amplifies the brand's message, weaving it seamlessly into the fabric of everyday discourse among their followers. Identifying influencers who resonate with your brand's ethos entails a meticulous vetting process, similar to finding an ally in a crowded room whose stories echo your own, whose audience mirrors your target demographic, and whose values align with the narratives you wish to propagate. This alignment ensures that the collaboration extends your reach and deepens your connection with an audience primed for engagement.

Negotiating collaborations transcends the exchange of terms and enters the realm of crafting a shared vision. It involves clear communication of goals, expectations, and boundaries, ensuring that both parties embark on this partnership with a mutual understanding and respect for each other's objectives and limitations. Effective negotiation strategies hinge on transparency, where the expectations regarding content creation, timelines, and compensation are articulated clearly, forging a foundation of trust and mutual respect. This process not only safeguards the interests of both the brand and the influencer but also sets the stage for a collaboration that feels less like an endorsement and more like a genuine recommendation, enhancing credibility and impact.

The co-creation of campaign content represents the heart of this partnership, where the influencer's creativity and understanding of their audience interlace with the brand's message, creating content that resonates authentically with followers. This co-creation process is collaborative, where ideas flow freely, guided by a deep understanding of the audience's preferences, desires, and pain points. It demands flexibility, allowing the influencer to infuse the content with their unique voice and perspective, thus maintaining the authenticity that endears them to their audience. This synergy ensures that the content feels organic and engaging and amplifies its reach, as followers are likelier to interact and share content that bears the hallmark of authenticity.

Measuring the success of influencer campaigns introduces a layer of precision to the art of collaboration, transforming subjective assessments of engagement into quantifiable metrics that reveal the depth and span of impact. Establish clear metrics rooted in the initial objectives of the partnership, whether they focus on increasing brand awareness, driving traffic, or boosting conversions. Tools and platforms that track engagement, reach, and conversion metrics provide the data necessary to evaluate the effectiveness of the collaboration. This evaluation extends beyond numbers, diving into the quality of engagement and the sentiment expressed by the audience, offering insights into how the partnership has shifted perceptions and behaviors. It's a detailed process where data guides the refinement of strategies, ensuring that future collaborations are more targeted, strategic, and resonant with the audience.

Where influencers have the power to shape perceptions and drive engagement, collaborations, and sponsorships, they represent a strategic approach for brands to enhance their presence and connect deeply with their audience. Through the thoughtful selection of influencers, transparent negotiation of collaborations, creative co-creation of content, and rigorous measurement of campaign success, brands can leverage the authenticity and reach of influencers to include their messages in the daily lives of an engaged and receptive audience.

6.3 HOSTING WEBINARS AND ONLINE WORKSHOPS

In digital marketing, where engagement is the currency and the marketplace is cluttered with varied voices and opinions, webinars and online workshops emerge as sanctuaries of connection and learning. These platforms offer more than just information; they provide experiences and moments where brands and audiences converge in real time, sharing knowledge, questions, and insights. The magic of these events lies not solely in the content delivered but in the community fostered during these interactions, a community that transcends geographical boundaries and unites individuals with shared interests and challenges. Coming together with a common problem to find a collective solution cultivates breakthroughs.

Topic Selection

Choosing topics for these digital gatherings is similar to curating an exhibition. Each piece displayed must captivate, educate, or inspire, drawing attendees into a deeper exploration of the subject. The selected topics should mirror the pulse of your audience's curiosity, addressing their surface-level interests and diving into the complexities of their challenges. This curation process involves an intricate data analysis, where insights from social listening, previous engagements, and industry trends paint a picture of the audience's needs. The most compelling topics promise transformation, offering attendees information and pathways to change, whether in their personal lives, businesses, or understanding of a subject. They promise to unveil expert knowledge, simplify complex concepts, or offer a new perspective on a familiar challenge.

Promotion Tactics

Promoting these digital events requires a multi-layered approach where organic and paid strategies intertwine to create a web of touchpoints with potential attendees. With its dynamic and interactive nature, social media is fertile ground for seeding interest and anticipation. When crafted creatively and precisely, organic posts act as an anchor, capturing attention and sparking curiosity. These posts, however, are complemented by targeted paid ads, precision tools that cut through the noise, reaching individuals whose interests align closely with the event's theme. This dual approach ensures a broad yet targeted reach, drawing in a diverse audience united by a shared interest in the topic. The promotion campaign is a crescendo of anticipation, building momentum through teasers, speaker introductions, and snippets of content, all leading up to the event.

Engagement Strategies

Maintaining engagement becomes most important once the stage is set and the audience gathers. The digital space, while ripe with possibilities, also teems with distractions. Strategies to maintain focus and foster interaction become the foundation of a successful event. Live Q&A sessions stand as pillars of engagement, transforming the unilateral flow of information into an exchange. Attendees can voice their queries and thoughts, feel seen and heard, and their engagement deepens. Interactive polls serve a dual purpose, offering insights into the audience's perspectives while keeping them actively involved in the content. These strategies, coupled with breakout sessions or interactive workshops for smaller groups, ensure that the event remains vibrant, the audience engaged, and the content resonant.

Monetization and Follow-up

While the immediate goal of webinars and workshops may be engagement and education, they also open avenues for monetization and lead nurturing. Monetization strategies vary, from charging a registration fee for exclusive content to offering premium, in-depth sessions post-event for a fee. Balancing the value provided with the cost ensures attendees feel their investment, be it time or money, yields substantial returns. The post-event follow-up process is critical, bridging the webinar's transitory experience and the brand's lasting relationship. This process involves a thank you message and a series of communications that nurture this growing relationship. Providing attendees with summaries, additional resources, or exclusive offers keeps the conversation going, gently guiding them from engagement to loyalty. This nurturing process is specific, requiring a blend of tact and strategy to transform attendees into leads and, eventually, customers.

In hosting webinars and online workshops, brands wield a powerful tool for connection, engagement, and education. These events offer a platform for more than just disseminating information; they provide a space for interaction, learning, and community building. From carefully selecting topics that resonate with the audience and the strategic promotion of events to the meticulous planning of engagement strategies and thoughtful follow-up, each step is crafted to enhance the attendee experience. When executed with precision and care, these gatherings not only elevate the brand's position as an authority in its field but also deepen the connection with its audience, fostering a community of engaged learners and loyal customers.

6.4 AFFILIATE MARKETING THROUGH SOCIAL CHANNELS

In the intricate web of digital commerce, affiliate marketing emerges as a strategy that joins the threads of collaboration, trust, and strategic promotion, creating a tapestry rich with opportunities for brands and creators alike. This approach, rooted in the symbiotic relationships between brands and their chosen affiliates, thrives on aligning values, audience expectations, and transparent communication. It's a balance requiring an eye for partners who augment the brand's reach and elevate its reputation and connection with its audience.

Choosing the Right Partners

The search for the ideal affiliate partners is a discerning approach, where the alignment between a brand's ethos and the affiliate's audience is paramount. This alignment ensures that the products or services promoted resonate deeply, not just as transactions but as solutions genuinely beneficial to the audience's needs and aspirations. It involves meticulous research into potential affiliates' content, audience engagement, and overall brand fit. Consideration must be given to those whose content ethos harmonizes with your brand, ensuring their recommendations carry weight and authenticity. This selection process is like cultivating a garden, where the right conditions foster growth and harmony, and choosing plants determines the garden's overall health and aesthetic.

Transparent Affiliations

In affiliate marketing, transparency is the cornerstone upon which trust is built. Today's Audiences are savvy; they seek authenticity and are wary of content obscuring its commercial intent. Therefore, it becomes crucial for brands and their affiliates to disclose the nature of their partnerships openly. This transparency is not only a legal obligation but a testament to the respect for the audience's intelligence and autonomy. It's about including this disclosure naturally into content, ensuring it informs rather than disrupts, maintaining the flow of engagement while honoring the audience's right to full awareness. This approach fosters trust, where recommendations are received openly rather than skeptically.

Effective Promotion Strategies

Crafting strategies for promoting affiliate products requires creativity and an intimate understanding of the audience's preferences and behaviors. It's about transcending the transactional nature of advertising, embedding product recommendations within content that entertains, informs, or inspires. Strategies include integrating products into storytelling, where their use or benefits are demonstrated organically within the narrative. Alternatively, creating content that addresses common problems or questions, with affiliate products presented as solutions, can offer value while subtly guiding the audience toward a purchase. This strategy ensures that promotions feel less like advertisements and more like genuine advice from a trusted friend. It's a nuanced art, balancing promotional efforts with the delivery of content that holds intrinsic value for the audience.

Tracking and Optimization

The deployment of tracking links and codes constitutes the backbone of affiliate marketing, providing a window into the effectiveness of promotional efforts. These tools offer insights into sales conversions and user behavior trends, such as click-through rates and engagement levels with affiliate content. This data is invaluable, offering a detailed map of what resonates with the audience and what falls flat. Optimization becomes a dynamic process where strategies are continually refined based on performance metrics. It involves adjusting content formats, tweaking promotional messages, or exploring new channels for affiliate marketing. This ongoing optimization ensures that affiliate marketing efforts remain agile, responsive to audience preferences, and aligned with the brand's goals. It's a meticulous process akin to sculpting, where data informs each stroke, gradually revealing the most effective strategies for engagement and conversion.

Navigating affiliate marketing through social channels, brands embark on a journey of collaboration, transparency, and strategic creativity. This journey demands a careful selection of partners whose audiences align with the brand's values and offerings, ensuring that promotions resonate deeply and authentically. Transparency in these affiliations forms the bedrock of trust, fostering an environment where recommendations are received with openness and credibility. The art of promotion, infused with creativity and a deep understanding of audience behavior, ensures that affiliate products are woven seamlessly into content that entertains, informs, and inspires. Finally, the intricate process of tracking and optimization ensures that strategies evolve in harmony with audience preferences and behaviors, maximizing the impact and efficacy of affiliate marketing efforts. In affiliate marketing, these elements amplify a brand's reach and deepen its connection with its audience, crafting a narrative of mutual benefit and shared growth.

6.5 CREATING AND SELLING DIGITAL PRODUCTS

In the digital marketplace, where the exchange of value transcends physical boundaries, the creation and sale of digital products represent a frontier brimming with potential. This domain invites a blend of innovation, insight, and strategic acumen, turning intangible ideas into coveted assets that address the nuanced needs of a global audience. The inception of these products begins not with a surge of inspiration but with an analysis of the audience's challenges, desires, and unmet needs. It's a process that mirrors crafting a bespoke solution, where the digital product, be it an eBook, course, or software, emerges as the answer to a specific problem, filling a gap in the market with precision and relevance. This ideation phase is critical, demanding a deep dive into audience data, feedback loops, and competitive landscapes to unveil opportunities for innovation that resonate on a personal level with potential customers.

Once the digital product takes shape, the focus shifts to strategies for its promotion and sale, leveraging the dynamic platforms of social media. This phase is akin to preparing the stage for a grand performance, where every element, from the script to the set design, is orchestrated to captivate the audience. With its myriad channels, social media offers a versatile stage for this performance, allowing for targeted marketing strategies that reach potential buyers where they are most engaged. Crafting compelling narratives around the digital product's benefits and unique value proposition, coupled with visually arresting graphics and videos, ensures the marketing message reaches the audience and piques their interest and desire to engage further. This targeted approach is supported by paid advertising, influencer partnerships, and organic engagement strategies, creating a multifaceted campaign that builds anticipation, fosters desire and drives action.

In bolstering the credibility of the digital product and tipping the scales from consideration to purchase, leveraging social proof becomes an invaluable strategy. Testimonials from satisfied customers, user-generated content showcasing the product in use, and endorsements from respected figures within the niche are powerful endorsements of the product's value and effectiveness. This social proof acts as a signal of trust, relieving potential buyers' hesitations and affirming the product's ability to deliver on its promises. It's a testament to the product's impact, transforming abstract benefits into tangible experiences shared by a community of users. Incorporating this social proof into marketing narratives across social media platforms amplifies the product's visibility and desirability, showcasing a narrative of success and satisfaction that attracts further interest and investment.

Optimizing the sales funnel for these digital products through social media insights represents the culmination of these efforts, turning interest into action and engagement into revenue. This optimization entails thoroughly analyzing engagement data across social media platforms and determining the most efficient channels, content formats, and messages that drive conversions. It involves refining the customer journey, from the initial touchpoint to purchase, ensuring that each step is intuitive, engaging, and without friction. Tailoring retargeting campaigns to recapture the interest of potential buyers who have engaged with the product but have yet to purchase and employing email marketing strategies to nurture leads, provide additional value, and gently guide them toward purchasing are pivotal in maximizing conversions and customer retention. This continuous cycle of testing, learning, and refining ensures that the sales funnel is not just a conduit for transactions but a nurturing path that builds lasting customer relationships, encouraging repeat purchases and fostering brand loyalty.

Creating and selling digital products is a foundational opportunity in the ample digital commerce space, inviting brands to innovate, connect, and grow. From the initial ideation of products that fill a specific market need to the strategic promotion and sale of these products via social media, each step is imbued with potential. Leveraging social proof and optimizing the sales funnel further enhances this potential, turning interest into engagement and revenue. This journey, while complex, is marked by the transformative power of digital products to meet the needs of a global audience, driving growth and fostering connections that transcend the digital divide.

As we transition from this exploration of digital product creation and sales into digital marketing strategies, the insights here serve as a foundation for understanding the intricacy of meeting audience needs, leveraging social media for targeted engagement, and cultivating a community of loyal customers. Though applied here in the context of digital products, these principles echo through the broader strategies that shape successful digital marketing efforts, guiding brands as they navigate the ever-evolving digital marketplace.

CHAPTER 7

AMPLIFYING ENGAGEMENT THROUGH VIDEO

In this business space where attention is the most sought-after currency, video is an anchor, laying the foundation of text and images with dynamic motion and sound. The allure of video marketing is not just in its ability to capture attention but in its profound power to convey stories, emotions, and complex ideas with immediacy and impact. From the silent films of the early 20th century to today's viral videos, the evolution of video as a medium underscores its unparalleled capacity to engage, entertain, and inform.

In digital marketing, leveraging video transcends traditional advertising; it invites audiences into a narrative, offering them a seat at the table, a glimpse behind the curtain, or a front-row ticket to innovation. The strategies surrounding video marketing—storytelling, live streaming, SEO optimization, and performance measurement—coalesce to reach audiences and resonate with them on a visceral level.

7.1 STORYTELLING THROUGH VIDEO

The heart of video's success lies in storytelling, a craft as old as time, now energized by digital innovation. Consider the impact of a well-told story at a dinner party—it captivates, entertains, and, more importantly, connects the teller to the listeners through shared human experiences. The same principles apply to crafting video content. Each video should serve as a narrative arc that guides the viewer through an experience, whether it's the journey of a product from conception to realization or a customer's transformation through a service.

Storyboard Template

This outline explains a structured framework for planning your video content, from the initial concept to the final scene. It encourages marketers to think critically about the story they want to tell, the emotions they aim to evoke, and the actions they hope to inspire, ensuring that every shot, every cut, and every word serves the greater narrative.

Live Streaming as a Strategy

Live streaming taps into the human desire for immediacy and authenticity. It strips away the polish of post-production, presenting brands and creators as they are and fostering a sense of intimacy and trust with the audience. The decision of when and where to stream should not be arbitrary. Timing plays a crucial role, aligning with when your audience is most active online, while platform choice should reflect where your community is most engaged.

Imagine a live Q&A session and the impact that would have on Instagram during a product launch, providing real-time answers to a curious audience or a behind-the-scenes look at an event on Facebook, bringing your audience along for the experience. These moments, raw and unfiltered, build a bridge between the brand and the audience, transforming viewers from passive consumers to active participants.

Video SEO Optimization

Just as a lighthouse must be seen to guide ships safely to shore, your video content must be visible to reach your audience effectively. Video SEO optimization ensures that your content is not just a droplet in the digital ocean but a guiding light that draws in viewers. This involves understanding the algorithms of platforms like YouTube, incorporating relevant keywords into your video titles, descriptions, and tags, and leveraging video transcripts to make your content more accessible and searchable.

Video inclusion on your website can boost your SEO, as search engines increasingly prioritize content that offers a rich user experience. Embedding videos directly on your site, accompanied by keyword-rich captions and descriptions, enhances engagement and signals your content's relevance and value to search engines.

Measuring Video Performance

Measuring the performance of your video content is critical to understanding its impact and refining your strategy for future content. Data remains supreme here. This involves tracking metrics, from view count and watch time to engagement rates and conversion metrics. Tools like YouTube Analytics offer a deep dive into how viewers interact with and see your content, providing insights into what captures their attention, keeps them watching, and compels them to act.

Video Performance Tracker

This interactive dashboard allows marketers to input critical performance data for their video content, visualizing trends over time and identifying patterns in viewer behavior. It is essential in making data-driven decisions about content direction, optimization strategies, and audience targeting, ensuring that your video marketing efforts are seen and felt.

In the digital era, video is a potent tool for storytelling, engagement, and conversion. Through strategic storytelling, the immediacy of live streaming, savvy SEO practices, and meticulous performance measurement, video content can transform how brands communicate, connect, and convert in the digital marketplace. As audiences' preferences evolve, video remains a steadfast medium through which brands can forge meaningful, lasting connections with their viewers, transcending the barriers of the digital screen to touch hearts and minds.

7.2 EMAIL MARKETING TACTICS FOR BUILDING LOYALTY

The artistry of email communication holds a pivotal place, wielding the power to transform casual browsers into loyal patrons. The canvas of an email allows for a level of personalization and engagement that, when executed with finesse, can weave a narrative that resonates deeply with each recipient. Herein lies the opportunity to elevate the mundane into the extraordinary, turning each email from a simple message into a tailored experience that speaks directly to the subscriber's heart.

Personalization Techniques

The magic of personalization in email marketing lies not in the mere inclusion of a recipient's name but in crafting content that mirrors their interests, behaviors, and preferences with uncanny accuracy. This level of customization requires a deep dive into the data that paints a portrait of each subscriber, from the pages they linger on your website to the products that catch their eye. With this insight, emails transform into personal letters, where offers, content, and calls to action align perfectly with the individual's current needs and desires. Advanced personalization techniques extend to dynamic content, where elements of the email shift to match the recipient's profile, ensuring that each interaction feels as though it were designed exclusively for them.

Segmentation Strategies

At the heart of effective email marketing is segmentation, which categorizes the vast sea of subscribers into distinct islands, each defined by unique characteristics and interests. This segmentation can be as straightforward as demographic factors or as nuanced as purchase history and engagement levels. By sending tailored messages to these segmented groups, the relevance of each email skyrockets, leading to higher open rates, increased engagement, and a deeper connection. It's akin to speaking directly into the ear of each subscriber, whispering messages that they're predisposed to listen to and act upon. This strategic segmentation ensures that resources are allocated efficiently, maximizing the impact of every email sent.

Automated Email Sequences

The power of automated email sequences unfolds over time, nurturing the relationship between brand and subscriber with strategically timed messages. These sequences, carefully crafted and triggered by specific actions or milestones, guide the subscriber from initial interest to deep loyalty. Welcome sequences introduce new subscribers to the brand ethos and offerings, setting the stage for future engagement. Re-engagement sequences breathe life into dormant relationships, rekindling interest with irresistible offers or captivating content. The beauty of these automated sequences lies in their ability to provide consistent, valuable touchpoints without manual intervention, ensuring that no subscriber falls through the cracks.

Measuring Email Success

In the array of email marketing, the compass that guides toward success is the meticulous analysis of key metrics. Open rates, click-through rates, and conversion rates serve as markers, indicating the health and impact of each campaign. Beyond these quantitative measures, qualitative feedback, gleaned from subscriber responses and surveys, offers a deeper understanding of the content's resonance. This dual approach to measurement illuminates the path forward, highlighting the strategies that captivate and convert. It's a continuous cycle of adaption and learning, where each campaign builds on the insights of its predecessors, driving towards ever higher levels of engagement and loyalty.

In the alchemy of digital marketing, email remains a potent element, capable of turning the lead of indifference into the gold of loyalty. Email marketing becomes a tool and a craft through personalization techniques, strategic segmentation, automated sequences, and relentless measurement. It demands creativity, insight, and a relentless focus on the subscriber experience, ensuring that each message reaches the inbox and resonates personally. In this connection between brand and subscriber, email marketing emerges as a powerful conduit for building lasting relationships and anchoring loyalty.

7.3 ADVANCED SEO TECHNIQUES FOR 2024

In the evolving theatre of digital visibility, where algorithms dictate the ebb and flow of online traffic, advanced SEO techniques emerge as the silent conductors of this grand symphony. Their application fine-tunes content melody to the receptive frequencies of search engines. It elevates the user experience, ensuring your website stands in the spotlight when the curtain rises.

Voice Search Optimization

In the digital era, where convenience is king, voice search optimization whispers secrets of untapped potential. As digital assistants become ubiquitous, the spoken word transforms into the key that unlocks the treasure trove of search queries. Adapting your SEO strategy to accommodate this trend involves a linguistic ballet, where questions posed in natural language guide the choreography of your content. This adaptation sees keywords expand into conversational phrases, anticipating the nuances of verbal inquiries. It's a detailed process where understanding the intent behind voice searches becomes as crucial as the words themselves, ensuring your content resonates in the echo of spoken questions.

Featured Snippets and Rich Snippets

In the visibility search, the pull of position zero on search engine results pages casts a long shadow. Featured and rich snippets can guide users directly to the most relevant, concise, and helpful information. A craft that structures information with clarity and precision is required to optimize content for these coveted positions. This involves the strategic formatting of content to highlight answers to frequently asked questions or to provide summaries of critical topics structured so search engines can quickly parse and present. Rich snippets, with their additional layers of information like ratings, prices, and availability, demand a structured data markup as a direct line to the algorithm, whispering the specifics of your content in a language it understands.

Mobile-First Indexing

With the ascendancy of mobile browsing, the principle of mobile-first indexing asserts itself as a hypothesis within SEO. This shift in priority by search engines, favoring mobile-friendly websites, heralds a new age where optimizing sites for mobile users becomes not just advantageous but essential. Ensuring your website is responsive, has fast loading times, and navigable on small screens is akin to rolling out a red carpet for users and search engines. It's an acknowledgment that the mobile experience is not a secondary consideration but the primary lens through which content is evaluated, consumed, and ranked.

Advanced Link-Building Strategies

Beyond the confines of on-page optimization lies the vast landscape of link building, a space where the currency of credibility is traded through the hyperlinks that bind the web. Advanced link-building strategies delve into creating connections that enhance your site's authority and standing in the intricate hierarchy of search engine rankings. This involves reaching beyond the conventional boundaries of guest posting and directory submissions to innovate in link acquisition. Crafting content that naturally attracts links, leveraging social media to amplify reach, and engaging in strategic partnerships for content syndication represent facets of a multifaceted approach. Each link acquired is a vote of confidence, a nod of recognition from one domain to another, signaling to search engines the worthiness of your content in the vast digital library.

In navigating the advanced SEO techniques of 2024, one embarks on a journey that transcends the optimization of content for search engines. It's a holistic embrace of strategies that aim for visibility and prioritize the user experience, recognizing that at the heart of SEO lies the simple yet profound goal of connecting users with content that best answers their queries, solves their problems, and enriches their digital experience. Through voice search optimization, the strategic positioning of content in featured and rich snippets, the prioritization of mobile-first indexing, and the innovative pursuit of link-building opportunities, the art of SEO in 2024 unfolds as a multifaceted endeavor. It challenges digital marketers to keep pace with the evolving algorithms and anticipate users' future needs and behaviors, ensuring their content remains visible and valuable in the ever-changing digital landscape.

7.4 UTILIZING CHATBOTS FOR ENHANCED CUSTOMER SERVICE

Where immediacy intersects with convenience, the emergence of chatbots as pivotal customer service tools unfolds a new chapter in digital marketing. These digital assistants, powered by the advances in artificial intelligence and machine learning, present an opportunity to redefine the boundaries of interaction between brands and their audiences. The deployment of chatbots across websites and social media platforms is not merely an adoption of technology but a strategic move toward creating a seamless, responsive, personalized customer service experience.

The initiation of chatbots into the digital domain of a brand requires a keen understanding of their potential to transform customer interactions. These AI-driven entities can provide instant responses to inquiries, guide users through websites, and assist in purchasing, thus elevating the overall user experience. The implementation process involves:

- Selecting a chatbot platform that aligns with the brand's specific needs.
- Customizing the bot's responses to reflect the brand's voice.
- Integrating it into the website and social media channels.

This ensures that the chatbot serves as an extension of the brand, providing consistent and valuable assistance to users across various digital touchpoints.

Customization and personalization stand at the core of a chatbot's ability to enhance the user experience. Beyond the basic functionality of responding to queries, chatbots offer the potential to deliver personalized interactions based on the user's history, preferences, and behavior. This level of personalization requires a sophisticated setup where chatbots can access and interpret user data to tailor their responses and recommendations. For instance, a chatbot on an e-commerce site can create products based on a user's browsing history or previous purchases, creating a highly personalized shopping experience. This not only aids in meeting the user's needs more efficiently but also creates a sense of understanding and being valued by the brand.

The integration of chatbots with Customer Relationship Management (CRM) systems amplifies their utility, transforming them into powerful customer service and support tools. By connecting chatbots to the CRM, every interaction a user has with the chatbot is captured, providing a wealth of data that can be used to enhance customer profiles, understand preferences, and tailor future communications. This integration ensures that chatbots contribute to the broader objectives of customer relationship management by providing insights that inform segmentation, targeting, and personalization strategies. Moreover, the data gathered through chatbot interactions offer valuable feedback on customer needs, pain points, and satisfaction levels, which can be leveraged to refine products, services, and marketing campaigns.

Analyzing chatbot interactions offers a window into the effectiveness of these digital assistants and their impact on the customer experience. Through analytics, brands can track response times, resolution rates, and user satisfaction scores, providing insights into how well the chatbot meets user needs and expectations. This analysis extends beyond quantitative measures, delving into the nuances of conversations to identify common inquiries, issues, and user sentiments. By examining these interactions, brands gain a deeper understanding of their audience, identifying opportunities to improve the chatbot's functionality, expand its knowledge base, and refine its conversational capabilities. This continuous cycle of analysis and optimization ensures that chatbots remain an influential and integral component of the brand's digital marketing strategy, adapting to changing user needs and technological advancements.

Chatbots represent a brand's commitment to providing timely, efficient, and personalized assistance in the dynamic interaction of technology and customer service. From their strategic implementation and customization to the integration with CRM systems and the meticulous analysis of interactions, chatbots represent a joining of innovation and strategy. They are tools for automation and catalysts for creating meaningful interactions that enhance user satisfaction, foster loyalty, and drive engagement. In this digital age, where the expectations of immediacy and personalization dictate the rules of engagement, chatbots are vital components of a comprehensive digital marketing strategy, closing the gap between brands and their audiences with every conversation.

7.5 IMPLEMENTING RETARGETING CAMPAIGNS

Retargeting emerges as a core principle mechanism, recalibrating the focus from broad-based casting nets to precision-targeted approaches that re-engage individuals who have previously interacted with a website but left without converting. This strategy holds the potential to transform fleeting visits into enduring customer relationships by reminding and persuading these visitors of what initially piqued their interest—retargeting lies in its ability to track these visitors through cookies and then display relevant ads to them as they navigate other parts of the internet. This creates a subtle but persistent reminder of the brand they encountered.

The initiation of retargeting campaigns begins with the meticulous segmentation of the audience. This process categorizes visitors based on specific behaviors, such as the products they viewed, the time spent on the site, or the stage at which they exited. This segmentation forms the bedrock of personalized ad experiences, ensuring the messaging is tailored to resonate with each segment's unique interests and preferences. For instance, a visitor who abandoned a shopping cart might be enticed by an ad highlighting a special offer on the items they considered. At the same time, someone who barely browsed a product category could be re-engaged with ads showcasing best-sellers or new arrivals in that range. This tailored approach enhances the ads' relevance and significantly increases the likelihood of conversion.

Within creative retargeting strategies comes innovation and pivotal roles in crafting ads that captivate without overwhelming. The creative decisions behind these ads venture beyond merely repeating what the visitor saw, weaving narratives, or presenting information that adds additional layers of value. Employing dynamic creatives that adapt based on the user's past interactions can significantly amplify the effectiveness of retargeting campaigns. Moreover, incorporating elements of urgency, such as limited-time offers or leveraging social proof through customer testimonials within these ads, can nudge the potential customer to purchase. The goal is to create a retargeting experience that feels personalized and beneficial rather than intrusive or repetitive.

The meticulous assessment of retargeting campaigns' ROI is critical to their success, guiding future strategies and optimizations. This evaluation encompasses a range of metrics, from click-through rates to conversion rates and beyond, painting a comprehensive picture of how effectively the retargeted ads are driving tangible outcomes. Tools and platforms specializing in ad performance analytics offer insights into the direct results of these campaigns and their impact on overall marketing objectives, such as heightening customer loyalty and brand recognition. By analyzing this data, marketers can fine-tune their retargeting efforts, adjusting factors like ad frequency, creative content, and segmentation criteria to maximize ROI. This constant cycle of analysis and optimization ensures that retargeting campaigns remain a potent tool in the digital marketer's toolbox, driving conversions and fostering long-term customer relationships.

In the tapestry of digital marketing strategies, retargeting campaigns emerge as both an art and a science, blending creative ingenuity with analytical acumen to re-engage visitors and guide them back to conversion. Retargeting represents a nuanced approach to nurturing potential customers, from the foundational work of audience segmentation to developing innovative strategies that resonate on a personal level and the rigorous ROI analysis to inform future efforts. It underscores the importance of personalization in the digital age, where successful marketing is about reaching broad audiences and making meaningful connections that drive engagement and loyalty. As we pivot from the focused strategies of retargeting to the different landscapes of digital marketing, the lessons learned here about precision, personalization, and performance measurement inform a holistic approach to engaging with audiences in a digital world where attention is fragmented, and competition is fierce.

Retargeting reminds us of the power of personalized marketing efforts to transform interest into action. By honing in on individuals who have shown interest but have yet to convert, retargeting campaigns are crucial in the digital marketing ecosystem, offering a strategic approach to increasing conversions and building lasting customer relationships. As we move forward, the principles underlying effective retargeting campaigns—personalization, creativity, and meticulous measurement—continue to inform broader digital marketing strategies, underscoring the importance of engaging with audiences in a meaningful and impactful way.

CHAPTER 8

DECODING THE MATRIX OF WEB AND SOCIAL ANALYTICS

Imagine a busy city market. Each stall, vibrant and alive with the hustle of commerce, represents a facet of your digital presence. The crowds of people weaving through, each with their tastes and preferences, are your audience. Now, envision having the ability to understand every interaction and every preference and tailor your offerings to meet the needs of this diverse crowd. This recognition is the power of web and social analytics - transforming raw data into actionable insights, equivalent to learning the language of your audience, allowing you to communicate with empathy and precision.

In this age, gut feelings are supplemented with complex data. Analytics tools serve as the compasses and maps that guide marketers through the complex landscape of user behavior and preferences. They are measurement instruments and lanterns illuminating the path to deeper engagement and growth.

8.1 OVERVIEW OF ANALYTICS TOOLS

Navigating the array of analytics tools available can feel like deciphering an ancient code. Each tool, from Google Analytics to Adobe Analytics, offers a unique lens through which to view your digital ecosystem. Social media platforms, too, bring their analytics into the mix, with Facebook Insights, Twitter Analytics, and Instagram Insights providing snapshots of engagement, reach, and more. The key lies in understanding which tools align with your specific needs, whether you're tracking website traffic, analyzing user behavior, or measuring the effectiveness of your social media campaigns. Selecting the right tools is like choosing the right spices for a dish; each brings flavor and enhances the overall outcome.

Analytical Tools

This chart outline guides you through the maze of analytics tools, comparing features, strengths, and use cases. It's designed to help you match your specific needs with each tool's capabilities, ensuring you have the tools needed for the particular date you're tracking.

The Importance of Data in Digital Marketing

In a realm where every click, like, and share holds significance, understanding the critical role of data in shaping marketing strategies is paramount. Data acts as the pulse of your digital presence, offering insights into what resonates with your audience and what falls flat. It tells stories of user journeys, preferences, and pain points, enabling marketers to craft experiences that meet and exceed expectations. The power of data lies not in its abundance but in its application - turning numbers into narratives that drive strategic decisions and foster growth.

Setting Up Analytics

The initial setup of analytics tools on your website and social media platforms is similar to laying the foundation of a building. It requires precision and foresight, ensuring that every piece of data you wish to track is accounted for. This setup involves determining what metrics matter most to your business, from page views and bounce rates to engagement and conversion metrics. It's about embedding tracking codes, configuring dashboards, and establishing baselines to serve as the benchmarks for your future growth. Remember, the goal of this setup is not just to collect data but to create a framework that transforms this data into actionable insights.

Interpreting Analytics Reports

Diving into analytics reports without clearly understanding what you're looking for can feel like being lost. The key to interpreting these reports is knowing which metrics serve as indicators of success for your business. It involves dissecting data to uncover trends, anomalies, and insights that inform your marketing strategies. For instance, a sudden surge in website traffic following a campaign launch confirms its effectiveness, while a high bounce rate on a landing page signals the need for optimization. Interpreting analytics reports is not a one-time task but a continuous process of exploration and discovery, where each piece of data holds the potential to unlock new opportunities for engagement and growth.

In this chapter, the exploration of web and social analytics unfolds as a journey through the matrix of digital data. From an overview of the diverse analytics tools at your disposal and the pivotal role of data in shaping marketing strategies to the foundational steps of setting up analytics and the art of interpreting reports, each element serves as a guidepost in the journey to understand and engage your audience with greater precision. This exploration is not about mastering tools or collecting data but about including this data into the base of your marketing strategies, transforming insights into actions that resonate with your audience and drive your digital presence forward.

8.2 SETTING UP AND TRACKING KEY PERFORMANCE INDICATORS (KPIS)

In this digital arena, Key Performance Indicators (KPIs) serve as the threads that reveal patterns of success and areas ripe for refinement. Identifying these KPIs requires understanding the broader objectives steering your digital marketing endeavors and the goals specific to each campaign. This process transcends selection; it aligns metrics with aspirations, ensuring every number tracked resonates with a facet of your business growth.

In the labyrinth of potential KPIs, discernment becomes crucial. For instance, if amplifying brand awareness is the cornerstone of your strategy, metrics such as website traffic, social media reach, and the volume of brand mentions stand out as relevant KPIs. Conversely, for objectives centered around engagement or conversion, metrics shift towards click-through rates, engagement rates on social media, and conversion rates from various digital campaigns. This alignment ensures that the KPIs chosen are not mere data points but beacons guiding toward your strategic north star.

Once the relevant KPIs have been identified, the next phase unfurls with the technical setup for tracking these metrics across your digital marketing platforms. This setup, intricate in its technicality, involves embedding tracking codes on your website, configuring analytics platforms to capture specific data points, and customizing dashboards to display these KPIs. This phase demands excellent attention to detail, ensuring every click, every interaction, and every conversion is captured and attributed correctly.

With the tracking mechanisms in place, the focus shifts towards benchmarking and goal setting. Benchmarking serves to map the terrain and understand the lay of the land based on past performance and industry standards. It involves an analytical dive into historical data, extracting insights illuminating paths previously treaded and heights previously attained. Against this backdrop, setting goals for your KPIs transforms into an exercise of precision. Goals are set not in the realm of aspirations but grounded in the reality of data, calibrated to stretch capabilities yet remain within the realm of attainability. This calibration ensures that each goal set is a step towards incremental growth, a marker for achieving your objectives.

The dynamism of digital marketing necessitates a system for regular review and adjustments of your KPIs. Far from a static construct, this system breathes life into your strategy, allowing it to evolve in response to data, market shifts, and consumer behavior changes. Having regular reviews scheduled to ensure that KPIs remain aligned with your current objectives, shedding those that no longer serve, and adopting new metrics as your strategies pivot. Adjustments, informed by data, are made not as reactions but as strategic maneuvers, guided by insights from ongoing analysis. This process embodies agility in digital marketing, where data informs decisions, ensuring your strategy remains fluid and responsively optimized.

The setup and tracking of KPIs unfold as an organization of strategy, technology, and analytics. Each step is foundational to crafting an informed and dynamic approach, from identifying metrics that resonate with your goals to the intricate setup required to track these KPIs across platforms. The benchmarking and goal-setting processes further refine this strategy, grounding aspirations in the bedrock of data and past performance. Finally, the system for regular review and adjustments ensures that your plan remains aligned with your objectives and adaptable to the ever-changing digital field. This approach to KPIs, rigorous in its methodology, ensures that every detail of your digital marketing efforts is calibrated for growth, engagement, and conversion, propelling your brand toward its strategic objectives with precision and insight.

8.3 USING DATA TO REFINE YOUR MARKETING STRATEGY

In the digital marketing matrix, data operates as the very lifeblood that propels strategies into the reality of precision and personalization. The age-old adage of "know thy audience" transforms from a philosophical musing to an actionable commandment under the lens of modern analytics. This commandment, powered by a vast pool of data collected across digital interactions, demands attention and a meticulous, data-driven approach to crafting marketing strategies that resonate on an individual level.

Data-Driven Decision Making

Navigating the digital marketing landscape with data as your guide shifts the paradigm from reactive tactics to proactive strategies. This shift entails a deep dive into the ocean of available data, extracting not just surface-level insights but diving deeper to uncover the underlying patterns and anomalies that signal opportunities for optimization. For instance, analyzing user engagement data across various platforms might reveal surprising trends in behavior that challenge preconceived notions, prompting a strategic pivot in content distribution or messaging. This approach, rooted in evidence rather than intuition, elevates decision-making from a game of chance to a calculated strategy, ensuring that data backs up every move and every plan is fine-tuned to the rhythms of audience engagement.

Segmentation and Targeting Based on Data

The art of segmentation and targeting finds its muse in the rich tapestry of data that web and social analytics reveal. Here, data acts as the scalpel that finely slices the broad audience into distinct segments, each characterized by unique behaviors, preferences, and needs. Data allows marketers to tailor their efforts, crafting messages and offers that align perfectly with the segmented audience's expectations. This targeted approach ensures that marketing efforts do not dissipate into the ether but strike the chord of relevance, significantly increasing the chances of engagement and conversion.

Personalization Strategies

The explanation of modern marketing lies in personalization - the ability to make each audience member feel seen, understood, and valued. Data is the cornerstone of personalization, offering insights that transform generic interactions into personalized experiences. By leveraging data on user behavior, past interactions, and preferences, marketers can create content and offers that cater to the individual's current needs and interests. This level of personalization extends beyond product recommendations, enveloping the user in an experience that feels seen and heard as if every digital touchpoint was crafted exclusively for them. The power of personalization, fueled by data, lies in its ability to cultivate deeper connections with the audience, turning fleeting engagements into lasting relationships.

Predictive Modeling for Marketing Strategies

As marketers, the ability to anticipate the future to predict the evolving needs and behaviors of the audience offers a competitive edge that transcends conventional strategy. Predictive modeling, rooted in data, emerges as the crystal ball of digital marketing, offering glimpses into future trends, preferences, and behaviors. This foresight is not born of mysticism but of algorithms, analyzing historical data to forecast future patterns. Predictive modeling allows for anticipating shifts in consumer behavior, allowing marketers to adapt their strategies proactively. For instance, by predicting the rise in demand for a product or service, marketers can adjust inventory levels, refine messaging, and align promotional efforts to capture the wave of interest at its crest. Moreover, predictive modeling can identify potential customer churn, offering an opportunity to intervene with targeted retention strategies. This forward-looking approach, powered by data, ensures that marketing strategies remain reactive to current trends and preemptively aligned with future developments.

The transmutation of raw data into strategic gold offers a pathway to engagement and growth previously uncharted. The application of data-driven decision-making, combined with the precision of segmentation targeting and personalization, craft a marketing strategy of unparalleled relevance and impact. This strategy, informed by data at every turn, ensures that each effort is a step towards deeper engagement, higher conversion rates, and a lasting relationship with the audience. In this domain, data is not just a tool but a guide, leading the way to a future where marketing transcends transactional interactions to create experiences that resonate on a profoundly personal level.

8.4 A/B TESTING FOR WEBSITES AND CAMPAIGNS

A meticulous approach to deciphering the preferences of a digital audience necessitates a method that transcends mere speculation, evolving into a structured experiment where hypotheses face the rigorous scrutiny of real-world interaction. A/B testing, or split testing, embodies this scientific spirit within digital marketing, offering a prism through which the impact of one variable against another is not just observed but quantitatively measured. The essence of A/B testing lies in its simplicity: two versions (A and B) are compared, which are identical except for one variation that might affect a user's behavior. This singular change could range from a headline, a call to action, a button color, or any element whose optimization could significantly uplift website performance or campaign efficacy.

The initiation of an A/B test demands an unambiguous understanding of its objectives, clarity that guides the selection of variables, and the definition of success criteria. It is not an indiscriminate application of change but a targeted exploration of how specific modifications influence user actions. For instance, an e-commerce site grappling with cart abandonment might hypothesize that a more prominently placed and color-contrasted 'Checkout' button could enhance conversions. In this scenario, the original button serves as version A, while the modified button becomes version B, setting the stage for an empirical comparison of their performance.

Designing practical A/B tests pivots on precise planning and meticulous execution. The process begins with identifying a single variable for testing, ensuring that any observed differences in performance can be attributed solely to this change. This focus prevents the conflation of results that multi-variable tests might introduce, providing the clarity and applicability of insights gained. Subsequent steps involve segmenting your audience to ensure a representative sample size for both versions, thereby enhancing the reliability of the test outcomes. The test duration is calibrated to accumulate sufficient data, balancing the need for timely insights with the statistical significance of the results. This phase is akin to setting the parameters of a laboratory experiment, where control, precision, and patience converge to yield findings of value.

The analysis of A/B test results transcends a preference for one version over another, diving into the why behind user behavior. Advanced analytics tools play a pivotal role here, offering a granular view of how each version performed against predefined metrics such as click-through rates, conversion rates, or any other metric crucial to the test's objectives. This analysis is not an aggregation of data but a nuanced exploration of user interaction patterns, seeking to unravel the reasons behind the superiority of one version over another. In this phase, the data speaks, revealing which version won and offering insights into user preferences, behavior triggers, and potential areas for further optimization. This ongoing commitment to experimentation creates an environment where decisions are data-driven, strategies are fluid, and user experience is paramount. Whether it yields expected or surprising results, each test becomes a stepping stone to deeper understanding and improved performance. This iterative process, where learning informs action and action fuels further learning, encapsulates the dynamic nature of digital marketing. It represents a commitment not to a finite goal but to the journey of constant improvement, where each insight gained is a stepping stone guiding future strategies.

A/B testing is a systematic approach to understanding and engaging the digital audience. Through the structured comparison of variables, the design and execution of tests, the analytical rigor in interpreting results, and the commitment to continuous optimization. It embodies the fusion of creativity and analytics, intuition and evidence, exploring the vast potential of digital platforms to connect, engage, and convert.

8.5 PREDICTIVE ANALYTICS FOR FUTURE MARKETING EFFORTS

Predictive analytics stands at the confluence where data's raw potential is refined into insights capable of illuminating paths forward, not just in hindsight but with foresight into future customer behaviors and preferences. These analytics transform historical data into a guiding path, projecting the likely outcomes of marketing strategies, customer engagements, and market trends with a degree of accuracy that borders on prescience.

Central to unleashing the power of predictive analytics is a deep dive into the toolbox of tools and techniques designed for this purpose. From regression analysis, which discerns relationships between variables, to machine learning models that adapt and learn from new data, the specific aspect of customer behavior dictates the tool one seeks to predict. For instance, cluster analysis might reveal distinct customer segments based on purchasing behavior, while time series analysis forecasts future sales trends based on historical data. Selecting the right tool requires a technical understanding of how these models work and an intimate knowledge of the marketing questions they're employed to answer.

Applying predictive analytics to refine marketing strategies is about deploying advanced tools and weaving the insights they generate into the fabric of marketing decisions. It's about moving beyond reacting to market dynamics to anticipating them, tailoring marketing messages, and personalizing customer experiences before trends shift or preferences change. This application demands a seamless integration of predictive insights into marketing workflows, ensuring that a deep understanding of future trajectories informs every campaign, content piece, and customer interaction. It also involves recalibrating strategies based on continuous feedback from predictive models, allowing for a dynamic marketing approach that evolves in lockstep with changing customer behaviors and market conditions.

Navigating the challenges of predictive analytics, from data quality and privacy concerns to the complexity of model selection and interpretation, necessitates a balanced approach grounded in best practices. Ensuring the quality and relevance of data inputs is paramount, as the accuracy of predictive outcomes hinges on the integrity of the data fed into analytical models. Balancing the granularity of personalization with privacy considerations is another critical challenge, requiring an approach to data usage that respects customer privacy while delivering personalized experiences. Additionally, simplifying the complexity inherent in predictive models—making them accessible and understandable to marketers, not just data scientists—is crucial for integrating predictive insights into practical marketing strategies. This balance is achieved through continuous learning, experimentation, and a commitment to ethical data practices, ensuring that predictive analytics drives positive engagement and value creation in marketing.

Predictive analytics is a pivotal element in contemporary marketing tools, offering a window into future customer behaviors, preferences, and market dynamics. Through the strategic application of this analytical approach, informed by a careful selection of tools and techniques and grounded in best practices, marketers can anticipate changes in the marketing landscape, tailoring strategies to meet future customer needs with unprecedented precision. This forward-looking approach, powered by predictive analytics, enhances marketing efforts' effectiveness and aligns them more closely with the evolving trajectories of customer behavior and market trends, setting the stage for the next evolution in digital marketing strategies.

CHAPTER 9

SOWING SEEDS OF ENDURANCE: CRAFTING CONTENT FOR TIMELESS IMPACT

Where trends rise and fall like the swiftness of ocean tides, the creation of evergreen content emerges as a baseline to withstand the internet fads. This content, resilient against the wear of time, is a perennial garden in the digital landscape, continuously attracting visitors with relevance and value. Like a well-tended garden that offers sanctuary and sustenance throughout the seasons, evergreen content provides a consistent, dependable source of engagement and income.

9.1 UNDERSTANDING EVERGREEN CONTENT

Defined by its timeless nature, evergreen content transcends the brief to address the core needs and questions that persist in your audience's minds. It's the answer to a query at 2 AM from someone knee-deep in a project, the guide for a beginner stepping into a new field, and the resource professionals bookmark for repeated consultation. This content type holds its ground amidst the ebb and flow of trends, offering value that doesn't expire with the calendar.

Strategies for Creating Evergreen Content

Crafting this content begins with deeply understanding your audience's perennial questions and interests. It involves digging into the core of your niche and identifying topics that maintain their relevance over time. These could range from 'How to Tie a Tie' to 'Tips for Basic Home Repairs'—topics that remain sought-after year after year. Developing these topics requires a blend of industry insight and keyword research, pinpointing the questions that endure beyond the moment's buzz.

A practical approach involves maintaining a content calendar dedicated to evergreen topics, ensuring a steady stream of content that continues to draw in an audience. This calendar acts as a blueprint, guiding the cultivation of a digital garden where each piece is carefully selected for its potential to thrive over time.

SEO for Evergreen Content

Optimizing evergreen content for search engines is akin to planting seeds in fertile soil, ensuring they receive the sunlight and water needed to grow. This optimization involves carefully selecting keywords that capture the essence of enduring topics woven seamlessly into the content's fabric. Meta descriptions and titles signal the curious clicker with the promise of timeless value, while internal links create a lattice of information, guiding readers through a garden of related topics.

The following points offer a straightforward guide to optimizing content for longevity. They cover keyword selection, meta optimization, and linking strategies. They serve as a tangible tool for creators aiming to anchor their content in the fertile ground of evergreen relevance.

Updating and Repurposing Evergreen Content

Regular updates keep evergreen content vibrant and ensure it evolves with its subject matter. This could mean refreshing examples, incorporating the latest statistics, or expanding sections to reflect new insights. Such updates enhance the content's value and signal to search engines its continued relevance, boosting its visibility.

Repurposing evergreen content into different formats—videos, infographics, or podcasts—extends its reach, adapting its timeless wisdom to the preferences of a diverse audience. This transformation allows the core message to flourish across mediums, planting it in various corners of the digital garden where different segments of your audience can discover and benefit from it.

In cultivating evergreen content, digital marketers find a strategy that ensures their efforts bear fruit long after the seeds are sown. This content, characterized by its enduring relevance, is a testament to investing in topics that resonate across time. Through careful selection, optimization, and regular revitalization, evergreen content becomes a part of the digital arena and a landmark, guiding visitors to a brand that understands and addresses their lasting needs and interests. In this way, evergreen content sustains a steady stream of engagement and income and cements a brand's position as a perennial source of value in the ever-changing digital domain.

9.2 SETTING UP AFFILIATE MARKETING FOR PASSIVE EARNINGS

Navigating the vast expanse of affiliate marketing will call for a discerning eye to recognize the symbiotic relationship between content creators and businesses seeking an amplified online presence. This digital alliance, rooted in promoting products or services, thrives on carefully selecting affiliate programs that resonate with the creator's ethos and the audience's interests. The criteria for this selection process transcend mere compatibility; they encompass a rigorous evaluation of the affiliate program's reputation, its payout structure's reliability, and its offerings' relevance to the creator's niche. It's a meticulous vetting akin to curating a gallery exhibit, where each piece displayed not only aligns with the curator's vision but also promises to engage and captivate the audience.

Once the affiliate programs align with the creator's content universe, the strategy shifts to seamlessly integrating affiliate links into content that informs entertains and subtly guides readers toward a potential transaction. This integration, far from being a blunt insertion of links, requires a finesse that weaves these references naturally into the narrative, ensuring they serve as organic extensions of the content's value proposition. Crafting such content demands a dual focus: on the one hand, it must stand firm in its ability to engage the reader on its own merits; on the other, it must subtly nudge the reader towards considering the affiliated offerings as logical solutions to their needs or desires. It's a delicate balance, where the presence of each element is felt but not overwhelming.

Conversion optimization takes center stage once the affiliate links are within the content. This phase scrutinizes the digital canvas of the webpage, paying particular attention to the layout, the strategic placement of calls-to-action, and the persuasive power of the copy surrounding the affiliate links. The goal is to create an environment that retains the reader's attention and encourages their journey from casual browsing to clicking on an affiliate link. It involves understanding visual hierarchy, guiding the reader's gaze through contrasting colors, compelling button designs, and copy that communicates the value of clicking through. This optimization is not a static setup but a dynamic, ongoing experiment that continually refines these elements based on reader interaction and conversion data, a process reminiscent of an artist iteratively refining a painting, each stroke informed by the last.

The tracking and analysis of the affiliate marketing performance measures the culmination of these efforts. Implementing tracking systems through the affiliate program's tools or third-party solutions provides a granular view of how each affiliate link performs, offering insights into click-through rates, conversion rates, and the overall revenue generated. This data guides future content and marketing strategies, highlighting which products resonate with the audience, which content formats yield the highest engagement, and which calls-to-action command the most clicks. It's a continuous cycle of analysis, learning, and application, where each piece of data sheds light on optimizing affiliate marketing efforts for maximum passive earnings. Through this lens, affiliate marketing transcends the mere act of promotion, evolving into a strategic endeavor that enhances the creator's revenue streams and deepens the relationship with their audience by connecting them with products and services that genuinely add value to their lives.

9.3 DEVELOPING AND SELLING ONLINE COURSES

In an era where knowledge is as sought after as tangible goods, the craft of transforming expertise into structured, digital courses represents a significant frontier for creators and educators alike. This digital transmutation of knowledge into accessible, scalable, and potentially lucrative online courses demands understanding one's subject matter and a strategic approach to its development, presentation, and distribution. The genesis of a successful online course lies in identifying and validating topics that not only ignite the instructor's passion but also meet the learning needs and financial willingness of a target audience.

Identifying profitable course topics requires a fusion of market research, audience analysis, and introspection. Creators must attune themselves to the whispers of demand within their niche—those questions perennially posed, skills universally sought, and gaps glaringly unfilled. This survey involves sifting through forums, analyzing search trends, and engaging directly with potential learners to distill a topic that resonates. Yet, validation extends beyond resonance; it demands evidence of willingness to invest. Surveys, pre-enrollment campaigns, and pilot programs serve as crucibles, testing the topic's viability against the market's realities. This process, rigorous yet revealing, ensures that the course conceived stands as a beacon for eager learners rather than a beacon that fades into the digital void.

Transitioning from concept to creation unveils a new box of challenges and considerations. The architecture of an online course—its structure, content, and delivery mechanism—calls for a balance between effectiveness and engaging presentation. Tools and platforms emerge as allies in this endeavor, from video editing software that brings lessons to life to course management systems that streamline the learning experience. Yet, the essence of creation transcends technology; it is the art of translating expertise into a narrative that educates, engages, and empowers. It requires crafting content that not only conveys information but does so in a manner that captivates and compels, utilizing multimedia, interactive elements, and storytelling to transform passive viewing into active learning.

With the course sculpted, attention shifts to the strategies that will escort it from obscurity to recognition. Marketing an online course necessitates a symphony of tactics, harmonized to cut through the din of digital content and captivate potential students. Email marketing campaigns, tailored and targeted, serve as personalized invitations into the world the course offers. In contrast, social media platforms offer stages for showcasing the course's value through snippets, testimonials, and live interactions. The essence of marketing lies not in the volume of outreach but in its resonance—crafting messages that echo the aspirations, challenges, and desires of the audience, making the course not just seen but sought after.

Amidst the myriad avenues for course distribution, the choice between hosting on one's website or leveraging established online course platforms presents a strategic fork in the road. Each path offers distinct advantages and considerations. Hosting on one's website affords unparalleled control over the user experience, branding, and pricing, cultivating a direct relationship with learners that can foster loyalty and upsell opportunities. However, this autonomy demands a readiness to navigate the complexities of e-commerce, from payment processing to user support. Conversely, online course platforms extend the reach of your course, placing it within a marketplace teeming with eager learners. They offer robust infrastructure and support but at the cost of transaction fees and competition with various other courses. Choosing these paths hinges on carefully weighing priorities—control and branding versus reach and convenience—guided by a clear understanding of one's goals, capabilities, and audience.

Developing and selling online courses in digital education unfolds as a journey marked by strategic decisions, creative challenges, and the transformative potential of sharing knowledge. From the initial identification of topics that bridge passion with demand to the nuanced art of course creation, marketing, and distribution, each step is a testament to the power of digital platforms to democratize education. This process, intricate and demanding, rewards not just with financial gain but with the profound satisfaction of enlightening others, extending the legacy of one's expertise far beyond the confines of traditional classrooms or mediums.

9.4 THE BENEFITS OF EBOOK PUBLISHING

Where information cascades through the web with velocity, the creation and dissemination of ebooks represent a beacon for knowledge seekers and a strategic asset for digital marketers. The ebook creation process, similar to alchemy, transforms raw expertise and narratives into polished gems of accessible wisdom. It begins with the detailed orchestration of content planning, where the scope and structure of the ebook take shape. This phase demands a keen eye for identifying topics that resonate with your audience's perennial queries and fill gaps in the existing digital library, ensuring your ebook is a sought-after resource.

From there, the journey ventures into the realms of writing, where the essence of your expertise is distilled into concise, engaging prose. This endeavor requires a balance between depth and accessibility, weaving complex ideas into a narrative that captivates yet educates, ensuring readers are informed and captivated. Following content crafting, the process transitions into formatting and design, where the ebook's visual aesthetics are honed. Critical for reader engagement, this stage involves selecting legible fonts, intuitive layouts, and compelling covers that beckon potential readers from their digital shelves. The design complements the written word and enhances the reader's journey through the ebook, making every page turn—or scroll—a pleasure.

The quest for the perfect self-publishing platform unfolds as a pivotal chapter in the ebook's journey from concept to digital bookshelf. The landscape of platforms, each with unique features and audience, demands a strategic selection process. Factors such as royalty structures, distribution reach, and format compatibility are scrutinized. Platforms like Amazon Kindle Direct Publishing offer vast audiences and seamless integration into the world's largest online bookstore. In contrast, others like Smashwords boast distribution networks that span multiple retailers, offering a breadth of exposure. Selecting the right platform is not merely a matter of convenience but a strategic decision that aligns with your ebook's goals, maximizing reach, revenue, or reader engagement.

With the ebook polished and published, attention shifts to the art of marketing, where the digital marketer's prowess is tested. Practical strategies for ebook promotion encompass a spectrum of tactics, from leveraging social media platforms to engage potential readers with snippets and teasers to harnessing the power of email marketing to offer exclusive previews to your subscriber base. Creative collaborations with bloggers, influencers, and other authors can amplify your ebook's visibility, creating a network effect that propels your ebook into the spotlight. Paid advertising, executed precisely on platforms where your target audience congregates, can drive significant traffic to your ebook's landing page, transforming curiosity into conversions. This multifaceted approach to marketing demands creativity with a data-driven mindset, where each campaign is measured, analyzed, and refined to optimize reach and revenue.

Beyond the immediate benefits of revenue and reach, ebook publishing offers a profound opportunity to build and enhance your author brand. This endeavor, transcending name recognition, involves cultivating a reputation as a trusted, authoritative voice in your niche. Ebooks serve as pillars of this brand, each publication reinforcing your expertise and deepening the connection with your audience. Engaging directly with readers through platforms like Goodreads or your blog can foster a community around your work, turning readers into advocates. Additionally, strategic branding involves consistency in your ebook's thematic elements and presentation style, ensuring that each publication is yours. This consistency, coupled with a commitment to quality and value, elevates your author brand, transforming it into a guiding light that attracts readers, publishers, and opportunities alike.

Where content is both king and kingdom, ebook publishing emerges as a strategic frontier for digital marketers and content creators. The journey from concept to publication, fraught with challenges and opportunities, demands creativity, strategic thinking, and a deep understanding of your audience. Through this process, ebooks transcend their role as vessels of information, becoming assets that enhance your digital presence, amplify your reach, and contribute to the ever-evolving narrative of your brand. Where adaptation and innovation are the currencies of success, ebook publishing stands as a testament to the power of content to inform, engage, and inspire.

9.5 INVESTING IN DIGITAL ASSETS

In the digital marketplace, assets transcend physical form, embodying value in pixels and URLs rather than brick and mortar. This shift has ushered in a new era for investors and creators, where websites, domain names, and digital products become the currency of choice. Each asset carries its unique allure, offering pathways to unfathomable passive income.

Websites stand as the digital equivalent of real estate, with their value hinging on location on the internet. The traffic they attract and the revenue they generate. Much like a prime piece of real estate, a well-positioned site can become a lucrative investment, drawing in visitors with its content, design, and utility. Similarly, domain names hold potential akin to undeveloped land, their worth often lying dormant until paired with the right project or idea. The most coveted domains are short, memorable, and brandable, resonating with simplicity and marketability. Digital products, encompassing everything from software to ebooks, represent a more fluid investment. Their value derives from their ability to solve problems, entertain, or inform, transcending physical limitations to reach a global audience.

The acquisition of these digital assets unfolds in various marketplaces, each tailored to the specific type of asset in question. Websites might change hands on platforms dedicated to digital real estate, where investors can assess metrics like traffic, revenue, and growth potential. On the other hand, domain names are often sourced from auctions or private sales, requiring a keen sense of future trends and brandability. Digital products might emerge from personal projects or collaborations, demanding development skills and a deep understanding of market needs.

Monetization strategies for digital assets vary as widely as the assets themselves. Websites might generate income through advertising, affiliate marketing, or direct sales, turning every visitor into a potential revenue stream. Domain names may be held for appreciation, sold to the highest bidder, or developed into full-fledged websites. Digital products, with their inherent scalability, offer the most direct path to revenue, sold to an ever-growing audience seeking solutions, entertainment, or knowledge.

Yet, the true potential of these assets lies not in their acquisition or initial monetization but in their careful management and growth. An asset neglected is an opportunity wasted, its value withering in the face of evolving market dynamics. Effective management involves regular updates, marketing efforts, and strategic development, ensuring that the asset remains relevant and continues to attract interest and revenue. Growth strategies might include:

- Expanding the asset's offerings.
- Improving its search engine visibility.
- Leveraging social media to widen its audience.

Success in digital assets is not guaranteed by mere acquisition but by thoughtful, strategic stewardship of these investments. It demands a blend of market insight, creativity, and perseverance, with an eye always on the horizon for emerging trends and shifts in consumer behavior. Yet, for those who navigate its complexities, the digital marketplace offers unparalleled opportunities for passive income and wealth creation, transforming ideas and foresight into tangible financial rewards.

As we close this exploration of digital assets, it becomes clear that the future of investment and income generation lies not in the tangible but in the digital, in the ideas and platforms that connect us across the vast expanse of the internet. From the enduring value of websites and domain names to the scalable potential of digital products, these assets offer a new frontier for those who want to grow their wealth in the digital age. The key to success lies in strategically acquiring, monetizing, and managing these assets, leveraging their potential to build a portfolio that generates sustained, passive income. These opportunities are as vast as the internet, limited only by one's vision and creativity.

As we move forward, we learn lessons from the digital assets populating the internet's landscape. Their potential for growth, management strategies, and paths to successful monetization serve as standpoints, guiding us toward the next chapter in our journey through the digital domain.

CHAPTER 10
ORCHESTRATING THE DIGITAL NOMAD SYMPHONY

In the modern workforce, 'digital nomad' has emerged as a term and a manifesto for a lifestyle untethered from the traditional confines of office spaces and geographical limitations. It's a testament to the era where the world shrinks to the expanse of a laptop screen, where work transcends borders and does so with a fluidity that challenges the notion of productivity. This chapter goes into the crucible of tools and strategies that enable this lifestyle, transforming the abstract into the tangible, ensuring that the freedom it promises does not devolve into anarchy of unmet deadlines and lost opportunities.

10.1 ESSENTIAL TOOLS FOR DIGITAL NOMADS

Picture a craftsman's workshop, with every tool diligently placed for optimal efficiency. For digital nomads, their toolkit is virtual, a carefully curated selection of applications and platforms that ensure tasks and projects are precisely managed. Tools like Trello for project management allow for a visual representation of tasks and deadlines, and the Pomodoro Technique, a method that divides work into focused intervals separated by short breaks, mimics the rhythm of traditional work environments within the digital space. These tools, when wielded with expertise, transform the nomad's workspace from a concept into a high-functioning reality, where productivity is not just maintained but amplified.

Integrating Tools into Daily Routines

Integrating these tools into daily routines mirrors the practice of a musician tuning their instrument before a performance. It's an act that requires consistency and mindfulness, ensuring that each day begins not with chaos but with a structured plan. It involves setting clear goals for the day, prioritizing tasks, and dedicating blocks of time for deep work interspersed with periods for rest and rejuvenation. This structure, far from imposing constraints, frees the nomad from the paralysis of unstructured time, allowing creativity and productivity to flourish.

Balancing Work and Travel

Balancing work with the allure of new destinations is like walking a tightrope, where the desire for exploration and adventure counterbalances focus and discipline. It necessitates a deliberate approach to planning, where work schedules are aligned with travel itineraries, ensuring that everything is maintained. Strategies might include:

- Selecting destinations based on connectivity and workspaces.

- Setting clear boundaries for work hours.
- Embracing local cafes or co-working spaces as transient offices.

This balance ensures that the nomad's lifestyle is sustainable, where work fuels travel, and travel, in turn, inspires work.

Avoiding Burnout

Burnout looms large in pursuing freedom, often exacerbated by the blur between work and leisure. Recognizing burnout signs and actively incorporating self-care and downtime strategies is crucial. This might manifest as dedicated days for disconnecting from digital devices, engaging in local cultural activities, or simply allowing oneself the luxury of doing nothing. It's a reminder that productivity is not measured by the constant ticking of tasks but by the ability to sustain creativity and motivation over time.

The Nomad's Toolkit

This explanation provides a comprehensive breakdown of the essential tools and strategies for digital nomads. It categorizes tools based on functionality—communication, project management, time tracking—and offers tips for integrating them into daily routines. Additionally, it outlines strategies for maintaining a balance between work and travel, highlighting the importance of setting boundaries and scheduling downtime. This breakdown is a reference and a blueprint for constructing a lifestyle where freedom and productivity coexist harmoniously.

In navigating the landscape of digital nomadism, the chapter articulates the tools and strategies essential for this lifestyle and underscores the ethos underpinning it. It's a narrative that includes the practical with the philosophical, challenging readers to reimagine where and how they work. It invites digital nomads to orchestrate their symphony, one where the notes of productivity and the rhythms of travel create a harmony that resonates with the promise of freedom and fulfillment. This chapter, dense with insights and strategies, serves as a compass for those who seek to chart their course in the unbounded expanse of digital nomadism, ensuring that their journey is not just feasible but sustainable, marked by growth, learning, and an unyielding sense of adventure.

10.2 AUTOMATING SOCIAL MEDIA AND EMAIL MARKETING

In the tapestry of digital nomadism, the strategic automation of social media and email marketing emerges as a tactic and a linchpin in sustained engagement and growth architecture. This digital alchemy, which transmutes routine tasks into orchestrated sequences of interaction, demands a discerning selection of tools—each serving as a cog in the larger machinery of digital marketing efforts. Discerning the optimal suite of automation tools involves navigating a landscape with options, each promising efficiency and effectiveness. From Buffer's streamlined social media scheduling capabilities to MailChimp's robust email campaign automation features, the key lies in identifying tools that not only automate but do so with an intelligence that mimics the nuanced understanding of a seasoned marketer.

The initiation of automation workflows stands as a rite of passage into a realm where time is not lost but leveraged. Here, the creation of workflows transcends mere scheduling, evolving into crafting a narrative that unfolds across digital channels, engaging audiences with a cadence that respects both their time and attention. This process starts with mapping out the customer journey, identifying key touchpoints, and designing sequences that guide the audience through this journey with the finesse of a skilled conductor guiding a performance. Effective workflows balance frequency with relevance, ensuring each automated message feels personalized and timely, not like a broadcast but a conversation.

Best email marketing and social media automation practices are not etched in stone but drawn from collective experience and experimentation. They dictate not a rigid adherence to rules but a thoughtful application of principles that prioritize the human element within digital interactions. This involves segmenting audiences with surgical precision to ensure that automated communications resonate on an individual level, crafting messages that reflect the brand's voice with authenticity, and testing different approaches to discern what elicits engagement and conversion. It's a practice that mirrors cultivating a garden, where understanding different plants' specific needs and tendencies leads to a more vibrant and flourishing ecosystem.

Measuring the impact of automation on marketing efforts unfolds as a quest for clarity in a sea of data. It's an analytical endeavor to quantify reach or engagement and understand the resonance of automated communications with the audience. Tools equipped with advanced analytics capabilities offer insights into open rates, click-through rates, and conversion metrics, serving as a compass guiding strategic adjustments. Yet, the accurate measure extends beyond these metrics, diving into the qualitative feedback from the audience, comments, and interactions that reveal the depth of engagement. This measurement is not a final judgment but a checkpoint in an ongoing refinement process, where data informs strategy and strategy informs content in a continuous improvement cycle.

In this gathering of automation within social media and email marketing, the digital nomad finds efficiency and a means to deepen connections with their audience, ensuring that each automated touchpoint is a step toward building a community engaged with content and the brand's ethos. This approach to automation, strategic and mindful, ensures that the digital nomad's voice echoes not as an echo but as a clarion call that resonates with clarity and purpose.

10.3 OUTSOURCING TASKS TO SCALE YOUR BUSINESS

Outsourcing emerges not merely as a strategy but as a lifeline, an essential recalibration of energy and resources that propels the business towards uncharted territories of growth and innovation. This recalibration requires a discerning eye capable of distinguishing between tasks that serve as the bedrock of your expertise and those that, while necessary, can be trusted by skilled hands beyond your immediate reach. Identifying these tasks hinges on evaluating both their strategic importance and the unique value you bring to them. It's a rigorous process, akin to a craftsman selecting which parts of their craft to execute personally and which to delegate, ensuring that every element, in-house or outsourced, resonates with the craftsman's signature quality and vision.

The quest to find and hire freelancers introduces a new chapter in this narrative, transforming the solitary pursuit of business growth into a collaborative journey. Platforms like Upwork and Toptal stand as digital crossroads where skilled professionals from diverse fields converge, offering their expertise to those ready to expand their horizons. Navigating these platforms requires clarity of purpose and vision, crafting job postings that not only describe the scope of work and expected outcomes but also resonate with the ethos of your brand, attracting freelancers who are capable and aligned with your vision. Interviews and trial projects further distill this talent pool, unveiling individuals whose skills and work ethic mirror your dedication to excellence. It's a vetting process, ensuring that each new addition to your team possesses the necessary skills and embodies the spirit of collaboration and innovation that drives your business forward.

Managing remote teams unfolds as a delicate relationship of trust and accountability, a balance between granting autonomy and maintaining oversight. Tools such as Slack for communication and Asana for project management are the conduits to achieve this balance, enabling seamless collaboration across time zones and geographical boundaries. Establishing clear guidelines and expectations forms the cornerstone of this management philosophy, outlining not just the what and the how of tasks but the why, imbuing each project with a sense of purpose and direction. Regular check-ins and feedback sessions become the custom of this relationship, creating a feedback loop that fosters mutual growth and learning. In this environment, remote teams thrive, driven not by oversight but by a shared commitment to the vision and goals of the business.

Maintaining quality control over outsourced tasks evolves into a continuous pursuit of excellence, an unyielding commitment to the standards that define your brand. This pursuit involves not just the establishment of benchmarks and quality checkpoints but also a culture of open communication and continuous improvement. Freelancers and remote teams are not only executors of tasks but partners in the creative process, their insights and innovations serving as catalysts for growth and refinement. Regular reviews of completed work, coupled with constructive feedback, ensure that each project meets and exceeds the established standards, reflecting the quality and excellence your business stands for. It's a collaborative effort where quality is not dictated but developed through shared goals, mutual respect, and unwavering dedication to the craft.

In this intricate tapestry of outsourcing, each thread - from identifying tasks to managing remote teams - weaves together to create a robust, dynamic, and expansive fabric. This fabric supports not just the immediate needs of the business but also its long-term aspirations, providing a foundation upon which the dreams of growth and innovation come to a realization. Outsourcing, in this light, becomes not a strategy alone but a transformation, a reimagining of what is possible when the boundaries of individual effort are expanded to encompass the talents and visions of others. It's a testament to the power of collaboration, where the sum of our efforts far exceeds what we could achieve alone, propelling the business towards new horizons of success and fulfillment.

10.4 BUILDING A REMOTE TEAM: HIRING AND MANAGEMENT STRATEGIES

Creating a remote team brings together talented individuals, each contributing their skills and expertise to strengthen your business. Constructing such a team involves navigating the dual realities of opportunity and challenge, where the liberty of geographical independence meets the necessity of cohesive collaboration. In this pursuit, the entrepreneur becomes both navigator and architect, charting a course through the complexities of remote work while designing a structure that supports seamless teamwork across distances.

Building a Remote Workforce

The initiation of a remote workforce is marked by recognizing its inherent benefits and challenges. The advantages extend beyond the flexibility of location; they encompass access to a global talent pool, the potential for round-the-clock productivity, and, often, a reduction in overhead costs. Yet, these benefits are counterbalanced by the hurdles of fostering communication and collaboration without the commonalities of shared physical space and the intricacies of managing diverse time zones and cultural differences. Overcoming these obstacles requires a blend of technology and technique, leveraging digital tools for communication and project management while cultivating an understanding of the nuances of remote work dynamics. This balance ensures that the spatial freedom afforded by remote work does not devolve into isolation but fosters a sense of connectedness and shared purpose.

Hiring for Remote Compatibility

Selecting individuals for a remote team transcends the evaluation of skills and experience; it goes into remote compatibility, where working independently, communicating effectively, and maintaining productivity outside a conventional office environment becomes essential. This selection process involves assessing technical abilities and discerning qualities such as self-motivation, adaptability, and self-management capacity. It also requires a clear insight into how a candidate's personality and work style align with the company's culture and values, ensuring that each addition to the team enhances its capabilities and enriches its collective ethos. The strategy for hiring thus becomes a multifaceted endeavor, combining structured interviews, task-based assessments, and in-depth discussions about expectations and work habits to identify candidates who are capable and genuinely compatible with the atmosphere of remote work.

Effective Remote Communication

The lifeblood of a remote team is communication, the underlying element that runs through the daily workings of daily operations, project collaborations, and social interactions. Effective communication in a remote setting demands more than exchanging information; it requires a deliberate effort to maintain clarity, prevent misunderstandings, and foster connections among team members who may never meet in person. Tools like Slack for instant messaging, Zoom for video conferencing, and Asana for project tracking serve as the conduits for this exchange, enabling real-time discussions, virtual meetings, and transparent monitoring of tasks and milestones. Yet, establishing communication protocols augments these tools' efficacy— clear guidelines on how and when to use each tool, the expected response times, and the etiquette of digital inter-actions. This structured approach to communication ensures that every team member can easily navigate the flow of information, contributing to a culture of openness and responsiveness that underpins successful remote collab-oration.

Fostering Team Culture Remotely

Cultivating a team culture in a remote environment is an exercise in intentional community building, where creating a shared virtual atmosphere compensates for the absence of a shared physical space. This cultivation involves not just the establishment of shared goals and values but the imple-mentation of practices that reinforce these elements in the day-to-day experiences of team members. Virtual team-building activities, from online game sessions to virtual coffee breaks, are crucial. Similarly, celebrating achieve-ments through virtual shout-outs, digital award ceremonies, or team highlights in newsletters reinforces a culture of recognition and appreciation. Moreover, encouraging open feedback and facilitating peer-to-peer mentorship further enhance the team's cohesiveness, creating an environment where learning, growth and mutual support flourish. This deliberate effort to foster team culture ensures that the remote workforce remains not a collection of isolated individuals but a unified team motivated by shared aspirations and bound by a collective identity.

In constructing a remote team, the entrepreneur embarks on a journey that transcends just a talent search. It is a venture into the heart of what it means to work collaboratively in an age where technology dissolves geographical barriers, creating opportunities for innovation, diversity, and growth. This endeavor, marked by the careful selection of compatible team members, the cultivation of effective communication practices, and the intentional building of team culture, is both a challenge and an opportunity. It is an opportunity to redefine work boundaries to create a team that is not just remote in location but connected in purpose, driven by shared goals, and sustained by mutual respect and understanding bonds.

10.5 LEGAL AND FINANCIAL CONSIDERATIONS FOR ONLINE BUSINESSES

Navigating the intricacies of legal and financial landscapes forms the backbone of a thriving online enterprise. This exploration into the legalities and fiscal responsibilities fortifies the business against potential pitfalls and paves a path for sustainable growth and international expansion. Understanding this framework is not just about compliance; it's about incorporating a fabric of trust and reliability around your digital presence, ensuring that every transaction and interaction is built on a foundation of integrity and security.

Understanding Legal Requirements

Boundless in its reach, the digital space is tethered to the tangible world by a web of legal obligations. These obligations encompass a spectrum of considerations, from the necessity of business registrations that anchor your enterprise in the legal landscape to the complexities of taxes that vary not just by country but often by region within those countries. Intellectual property rights, too, stand as sentinels guarding the uniqueness of your offerings, ensuring that the innovations and creations that distinguish your brand are protected under the aegis of law. This legal maze, daunting though it may appear, offers a roadmap for navigating the difficulties of online entrepreneurship, ensuring that your business not only survives but thrives in the global marketplace.

Setting Up Business Finances

The financial health of an online business is akin to the circulatory system of a living organism, essential not just for survival but for growth. Setting up this financial system involves more than merely tracking income and expenses; it demands understanding accounting practices that ensure compliance, efficiency, and transparency. Revenue tracking becomes a critical tool in this endeavor, offering insights into the financial pulse of the enterprise. In contrast, financial forecasting allows for strategic planning, anticipating challenges, and seizing opportunities in the ever-evolving digital market. This financial backbone supports not just the day-to-day operations but also the long-term aspirations of the business, ensuring that every decision and every investment is grounded in fiscal prudence and strategic foresight.

Protecting Your Business

Where transactions transcend physical boundaries, protecting your business and your customers becomes foundational. This protection is twofold, encompassing not just the physical security of data through cybersecurity measures but also the legal security afforded by contracts, privacy policies, and terms of service. These legal instruments serve as a shield and sword, defending against potential infringements while ensuring the business operates within a transparency and accountability framework. The importance of these protections cannot be overstated; they form the wall against which internal and external threats are measured and mitigated, ensuring that the trust placed in your business by customers and partners is well-founded and maintained.

Navigating International Business Considerations

The allure of the global market is undeniable, offering various opportunities created from the diverse threads of international audiences. Yet, this expansion brings a complex array of considerations, from the fluctuations of currency exchange that impact pricing and profitability to the labyrinth of tax obligations that vary with each jurisdiction. In their pursuit of global reach, the digital nomad must also contend with international laws that govern e-commerce, data protection, and consumer rights. These considerations demand not just awareness but adaptability, the ability to pivot strategies in response to the shifting sands of international commerce. It's a balance, maintaining the agility of a small enterprise while navigating the complexities of a global player.

In wrapping up this exploration into the legal and financial scaffolding that supports an online business, it becomes evident that these considerations are more than hurdles to overcome. They are the very backbone that connects the vision of digital entrepreneurship with the reality of a sustainable, thriving enterprise. From the legal frameworks that ensure compliance and protection to the financial systems that underpin growth and stability, these elements together form a cohesive whole. They are the unseen forces that shape the trajectory of an online business, guiding it through the challenges of today and toward the opportunities of tomorrow. As we shift forward, it's with the understanding that the journey of digital entrepreneurship is one of continuous learning and adaptation, a path marked by challenges but illuminated by the boundless potential of the digital age.

CHAPTER 11

NAVIGATING THE FUTURE OF DIGITAL MARKETING

The digital marketing landscape is like a river, constantly flowing and changing with each new technological advancement and cultural shift. For marketers, staying afloat means paddling harder and smarter, anticipating the next bend or rapid before it arrives. This foresight is not a gift but a skill honed through diligent observation, analysis, and the willingness to adapt strategies in real-time. In this constantly evolving environment, trends are both the current propels forward and the undertow that can drag down the unwary.

11. 1 PROACTIVE TRENDSPOTTING

Like a surfer scanning the horizon for the next big wave, marketers must keep their eyes peeled on the horizon of digital marketing, identifying emerging trends before they break. This vigilance involves a blend of tools and resources, from in-depth industry reports that chart the progress of new technologies to social listening tools that capture the whispers of change in consumer behavior.

Imagine attending a major industry conference where keynote speakers highlight innovations on the cusp of mainstream adoption. Here, amidst the buzz and energy, notes taken and connections made become the seeds of future marketing strategies. The key lies in critically collecting and analyzing this information and selecting between fleeting fads and trends with the momentum to reshape the marketing landscape.

Analyzing Impact

With a trend on the horizon, the next step involves assessing its potential impact. This analysis is akin to a chef tasting a dish as it cooks, determining what ingredients it needs. Marketers must ask: How will this trend affect our target audience's behavior? What opportunities does it present for engagement, and what threats might it pose to our current strategies? For instance, the rise of voice search necessitates shifting toward more natural language in SEO strategies, which could redefine the landscape of search engine results pages. This phase requires a willingness to experiment, running small-scale tests to gauge the trend's effect on engagement and conversion rates. It's about making informed hypotheses and having the flexibility to pivot based on the data gathered.

Case Studies of Trend Adaptation

Insight and inspiration often come from those who've navigated the path before us. Brand case studies that have successfully adapted to emerging trends offer valuable lessons. Consider a brand that seamlessly integrated augmented reality (AR) into its marketing strategy, allowing customers to visualize products in their homes before purchasing. This adaptation capitalized on the trend toward immersive experiences and addressed a practical need, significantly boosting conversion rates. Each case study serves as a blueprint, highlighting the successes and challenges faced and overcome. These narratives underscore the importance of agility in strategy and the value of innovation in maintaining relevance and competitiveness.

Future-proofing Strategies

The ultimate goal of trendspotting and analysis is to develop strategies that stand the test of time. Future-proofing in digital marketing is less about predicting the future with certainty and more about building resilience in marketing strategies, ensuring they can adapt to changes with minimal disruption. This process involves diversifying marketing channels to avoid over-reliance on any single platform, investing in evergreen content that remains relevant regardless of trends, and fostering a culture of continuous learning within marketing teams. It's about creating a foundation strong enough to support rapid pivots and innovation, ensuring the business is ready to shift when the landscape shifts, and surviving and thriving in the new environment.

The Trendspotter's Toolkit

This breakdown distills the essence of proactive trendspotting into a layout designed for marketers at all levels. It outlines the essential tools and resources for identifying emerging trends, from industry reports and conferences to social listening platforms. Additionally, it analyzes the impact of identified trends, incorporating experimentation and data analysis. Case studies are summarized with key takeaways highlighted, providing actionable insights. This allows marketers to have a base level of resilience. It's not just a resource but a catalyst for innovation, encouraging marketers to look beyond the horizon and confidently navigate the future of digital marketing.

11.2 LEARNING NEW SKILLS: ONLINE RESOURCES AND COURSES

Innovation and change are the only constants. Acquiring new skills is more than just professional development—it becomes a survival strategy. Nurturing one's skill set amidst this ever-evolving demands dedication and a strategic learning approach that aligns with immediate job requirements and future career aspirations. This necessity brings forth an exploration of online learning platforms, those repositories of knowledge where expertise is not constrained by geography or institution but is freely accessible to those desiring to learn.

Navigating the plethora of online resources available for upskilling in digital marketing begins with discerning the quality and relevance of the content. Massive Open Online Courses (MOOCs), offered by platforms such as Coursera and edX, offer courses designed by renowned universities and industry leaders, providing insights into foundational concepts and cutting-edge strategies. Simultaneously, specialized industry platforms like the Google Digital

Garage and HubSpot Academy focus on practical, tool-specific training, eliminating the gap between theoretical knowledge and real-world application. Selecting the right platform involves weighing the depth and breadth of the content against the specificity and applicability of the skills taught. It's a balance between acquiring a broad under-standing of digital marketing principles and mastering the tools and techniques to drive immediate results in one's work.

Skill prioritization emerges as a critical task in this learning journey. The digital marketing domain's myriad disciplines—from SEO and content marketing to data analytics and social media strategy—present a landscape rich with learning opportunities. Yet, not all skills hold equal value at every stage of a marketer's career. Prioritization, therefore, hinges on assessing current competencies, job demands, and industry trends, identi-fying areas where skill development can fill gaps and propel career growth.

Staying updated on digital marketing tools, technologies, and methodologies requires continuous learning. The pace at which new platforms emerge and algorithms change renders yesterday's best practices obsolete, demanding an agile approach to professional development. Subscribing to industry newsletters, participating in webinars, and joining professional forums or masterminds keep marketers at the forefront of industry developments. Moreover, engaging with a community of peers provides insights into emerging trends and diverse perspectives that can challenge and refine one's understanding of digital marketing strategies. This commitment transforms learning from a task to be completed into a habit to be cultivated, ensuring one's skills remain sharp and relevant.

Implementing learning into practice stands as the ultimate test of the efficacy of one's educational endeavors, but more so personal development pathway. The transition from theory to application, from learning to doing, is where the value of new knowledge is realized. This phase often involves experimenting with new strategies within the safe confines of pilot projects, allowing for assessing outcomes without the risk of widespread impact. A/B testing, for instance, becomes a powerful tool for evaluating the effectiveness of new tactics, providing data-driven insights that can guide broader strategic decisions. Additionally, sharing newfound knowledge with colleagues not only reinforces one's learning but also enhances the collective skill set of the team, fostering an environment where innovation thrives. It's a process that blurs the line between learning and doing, where each new skill acquired immediately finds application, validating its value and encouraging further exploration. Witnessing these skills building upon one another is the ultimate sense of satisfaction, reminding you why you began the journey in the first place.

In this continuous cycle of learning and application, digital marketers find professional growth and a sense of fulfillment. Acquiring new skills becomes a journey marked by milestones of achievement and discovery, each step forward revealing new horizons to explore. This is a testament to the transformative power of learning, where the pursuit of knowledge becomes the key to navigating the complexities within the space, ensuring that one remains competent and competitive in an ever-changing field.

11.3 NETWORKING AND COLLABORATING WITH OTHER DIGITAL MARKETERS

Digital marketing's boundaries are constantly redrawn; weaving networks with peers transcends social interaction. It becomes a pivotal strategy, a conduit for innovation and growth. Cultivating rich connections with other digital marketers is not about collecting contacts but fostering relationships that spark creativity, challenge ideas, and open doors to unforeseen opportunities. New insights are born in these intersections of knowledge and experience, illuminating paths previously unimagined.

Building a Professional Network

Constructing a professional network in the digital marketing sphere requires a blend of strategic outreach and genuine engagement. Initiating conversations at virtual conferences, participating actively in industry webinars, and contributing thoughtfully to online communities sets the groundwork. No matter how minor it may seem, each interaction plants the seeds for a meaningful professional relationship. Over time, regular nurturing through consistent engagement and mutual support transforms these initial connections into a thriving ecosystem of professional allies. This garden of connections serves as a reservoir of knowledge, support, and opportunity, ready to be tapped when the need arises.

Collaboration Opportunities

With its many challenges and opportunities, digital marketing often reveals moments ripe for collaboration. Identifying these opportunities requires an attuned sense of one's strengths and the complementary skills of others within the network. Perhaps a project demands expertise in an area outside one's purview, or a new marketing trend emerges, necessitating a joint exploration. These collaborations, formalized in joint ventures or informal partnerships for a specific campaign, act as crucibles for innovation. They are the fertile ground from which new ideas sprout, are tested, and refined through each collaborator's diverse perspectives and expertise. Through these partnerships, projects benefit from combined skill sets and offer a unique opportunity for learning and growth, pushing the boundaries of what can be achieved in isolation.

Leveraging Online Communities

Online communities, social media groups, and industry associations offer vibrant platforms for networking and collaboration. These digital congregations are watering holes where digital marketers from various niches gather, drawn by shared interests and common goals. Engaging in these communities intending to contribute, rather than extracting value, creates an atmosphere of reciprocity. Sharing insights on a perplexing SEO challenge, offering advice on social media strategies, or contributing to discussions about emerging digital tools elevates the community's collective knowledge. It cements one's reputation as a valuable member. This reciprocity is the currency of online communities, facilitating deeper connections and opening avenues for collaboration that extend beyond the digital confines of the community or group.

Mentorship and Guidance

The roles of mentor and mentee are fluid, with knowledge and experience flowing freely in both directions. Seeking out mentors offers a pathway for navigating the complexities of the field, providing clarity and direction amidst the constant change. With their wealth of experience and insights, these mentors act as guides, offering answers and challenging questions that provoke deeper understanding and growth. Conversely, becoming a mentor to others is an investment in the future of the field, an opportunity to give back and shape the next generation of digital marketers. This formal or informal mentorship is a testament to the power of shared knowledge and the collective advancement of the field. It underscores the understanding that growth is not a zero-sum game but a communal endeavor where success is amplified through the success of others.

In this intricacy of networking and collaboration, digital marketers find both allies and inspiration. The connections forged and nurtured today become the collaborative ventures of tomorrow, driving innovation and pushing the envelope of what's possible. Through these relationships, the field of digital marketing continues to evolve, propelled not just by individual ambition but by a shared commitment to exploration, learning, and mutual success.

Holistic Personal Development

In digital marketing, where the technical intertwines with the creative, cultivating a well-rounded persona becomes pivotal. This holistic approach to personal development is far more than just acquiring hard skills and venturing into soft skills, leadership prowess, and emotional intelligence. Each component acts as a cog in the intricate machinery of a successful career, where the ability to communicate effectively, lead with empathy, and navigate the emotional landscapes of oneself and others marks the difference between mediocrity and excellence. The art of persuasion, critical in crafting compelling narratives, hinges not just on the logical appeal but significantly on the emotional resonance, making emotional intelligence not an optional add-on but a cornerstone of marketing success. Similarly, leadership abilities, often misconstrued as relevant only in managerial roles, are indispensable across all levels. They empower individuals to take initiative, inspire team creativity, and drive projects with a vision that transcends the confines of job descriptions. Therefore, this holistic development is not pursued in isolation but woven into the fabric of daily work life, where each interaction and challenge becomes an opportunity for growth and refinement.

Work-life Balance

The digital marketer's odyssey is faced with the peril of burnout, a shadow that casts large over the landscape of endless deadlines and constant connectivity. Maintaining a healthy work-life balance emerges as a strategy for personal well-being and a critical factor in sustaining long-term productivity and creativity. This equilibrium requires more than time management; it demands a conscious allocation of resources to activities that rejuvenate the spirit and rekindle the spark of creativity. It might manifest as a hobby that provides a creative outlet separate from work or physical activity that invigorates the mind as much as it does the body. More fundamentally, it involves setting boundaries around work hours and digital consumption, creating silence amidst the noise, where the mind can wander, reflect, and rest. In these moments of disconnection, the wellspring of creativity becomes replenished, ensuring that one returns to work not just rested but reinvigorated, with a renewed perspective that enriches both the quality of work and the quality of life.

Adapting to Change

Change is the only constant in this domain, a relentless tide that reshapes the landscape with each technological innovation and cultural shift. Navigating this flux requires adaptability and resilience, cultivated not in the face of change but in anticipation. It involves staying attuned to the undercurrents of the industry, recognizing the signs of impending shifts, and preparing to pivot strategies with agility. This anticipation is not a passive waiting but an active preparation, building a repertoire of skills and knowledge applied across various scenarios. In this context, resilience is forged in the fires of challenge, where setbacks are viewed not as obstacles but as stepping stones and opportunities to learn and grow stronger. This mindset transforms the uncertainty of change from a source of anxiety into a catalyst for innovation, driving one to explore uncharted territories with confidence and genuine curiosity.

Continuous Improvement Mindset

At the heart of a sustainable career in digital marketing lies the spirit of continuous improvement, a pursuit of excellence that is more than the satisfaction of current achievements. This mindset is characterized by openness to feedback, a drive for learning, and a genuine curiosity about the ever-evolving space. It propels one to seek formal educational opportunities and learn from every project and every campaign, extracting lessons from successes and failures. This approach fosters an environment where feedback is not feared but welcomed, seen as a stepping stone guiding towards greater effectiveness and impact. Moreover, it instills a habit of self-reflection, regularly auditing one's work and strategies critically, always asking, "How can this be better?" This continuous loop of learning, applying, and evaluating ensures one's skills and strategies remain relevant and cutting-edge, driving innovation and setting new benchmarks in digital marketing.

11.5 CREATING A PERSONAL LEARNING PLAN

A personal learning plan is necessary for those aspiring to navigate and shape these terrains. This blueprint for educational pursuit, far from just a checklist of skills to acquire, embodies a strategic approach to professional and personal evolution. It begins with delineating clear, actionable learning objectives that resonate with current industry demands and the pulsing beat of one's career aspirations.

These goals, set against the backdrop of emerging trends and technological advancements, serve as guiding stars in the vast expanse of knowledge, ensuring that every step taken is a step towards relevance and excellence.

Customizing one's learning trajectory becomes an exercise in self-reflection and strategic planning. It demands an intimate understanding of one's rhythms and routines, preferences in consuming knowledge—through the written word, auditory stimulation, or visual demonstrations—and the realities of one's schedule. This path, tailored to fit the contours of individual learning styles and the constraints of daily obligations, ensures that the pursuit of knowledge becomes not a burden but a seamlessly integrated aspect of everyday life. It's in this customization that learning surpasses obligation and morphs into a journey of discovery and empowerment.

Tracking progress along this carefully charted course necessitates a system that monitors milestones reached and illuminates areas needing further exploration or reinforcement. This system, akin to the navigational tools of an explorer, employs a variety of mechanisms—from digital platforms that log learning hours to journals that capture reflections and insights gained. This ongoing assessment acts as a mirror reflecting the journey thus far and a map showing the terrain yet to be traversed. It offers the dual benefit of motivating continued pursuit through visible achievements and providing flexibility to adjust the learning plan in response to evolving goals or unforeseen challenges.

The assembly of resources and tools to support this educational voyage is essential. This collection, from the vast repositories of knowledge in books and scholarly articles to the dynamic worlds of podcasts and webinars, forms the bedrock of the learning experience. It also spans the range of online courses offering structured learning paths and forums where insights and queries are exchanged with peers and mentors. This arsenal of educational tools, curated with discernment, ensures that the learner is well-equipped to tackle the complexities of digital marketing, armed not just with theoretical knowledge but with practical insights and the wisdom gleaned from shared experiences. It provides clarity amidst the chaos of constant change, ensuring that with each new skill mastered and insight gained, they are better poised to respond to the present demands and shape future trends. Therefore, this plan becomes more than a guide—it becomes a compass, ensuring that the marketer remains relevant and revolutionary no matter how the digital landscape may shift.

Navigating through the digital era's complex web, crafting a personal learning plan stands out as a testament to the power of intentional learning. It underlines the importance of setting precise goals, tailoring learning paths to individual needs, meticulously tracking progress, and compiling a robust array of resources. This approach ensures the continuous development of crucial skills. It keeps the marketer at the forefront of innovation, ready to adapt and excel in this digital marketing space. As we move forward, this commitment to lifelong learning and adaptability sets the foundation for individual success and advancing the digital marketing field at large.

CHAPTER 12

NAVIGATING THE NEXT WAVE OF SOCIAL MEDIA MARKETING

Social media is a dynamic giant in the digital marketing environment; its echoes spread across the expanse of consumer interactions and brand narratives. Ever fluid, this domain commands an understanding and agile approach to harness its evolving potential. The future of social media marketing, akin to predicting weather patterns in an unpredictable climate, demands a keen sense of observation, analysis, and adaptability. Herein, we explore the facets of this evolution, touching upon the trends poised to shape the terrain, the integration of developing platforms promising early-mover advantages, the change of content formats aligning with audience preferences, and the custom relationship between personalization and privacy.

12.1 PREDICTING SOCIAL MEDIA TRENDS

Forecasting the trajectory of social media trends necessitates a thorough analysis of current movements and consumer behaviors. Imagine sitting at a café, observing people engrossed in their devices. This scene, commonplace today, was unfathomable two decades ago. The rapid adoption of technology and its integration into daily life hint at future patterns. For instance, the increasing concern over mental health and digital well-being could steer platforms towards more meaningful, less intrusive engagement models. Tools like social listening platforms and analytics software serve as the radar in this endeavor, capturing signals of changing winds. They provide data-driven insights into what content resonates, shifts in platform usage, and emerging communication preferences, allowing marketers to anticipate and align with future consumer expectations.

Integrating Emerging Platforms

This is a fertile ground for new platforms, each introducing novel paradigms for connection and interaction. Early adoption of these platforms into a marketing strategy can offer substantial benefits, setting a brand apart uniquely. Consider the advent of TikTok and how quickly it became a powerhouse for user-generated content and viral trends. Brands that recognized its potential early on were able to carve out significant presence and engagement. The key lies in identifying platforms that align with a brand's voice and audience demographics. This strategic alignment and creative, platform-specific content amplify reach and strengthen brand identity among early adopters and beyond.

Evolving Content Formats

The evolution of the content format on social media is a testament to the shifting landscapes of consumer attention and engagement. The rise of short-form videos, spearheaded by platforms like TikTok and Instagram Reels, underscores a preference for digestible, engaging content that delivers value within minutes or seconds. This trend challenges brands to rethink content creation, focusing on storytelling that captivates and conveys messages succinctly. Similarly, interactive content such as polls, quizzes, and AR filters fosters a two-way dialogue, transforming passive viewers into active participants. Adapting to these formats requires creativity and understanding of the underlying technology, ensuring that content entertains and seamlessly integrates with the user experience.

Privacy and Personalization

The closeness of privacy and personalization within social media marketing paints a complex picture. On one side, there's an escalating demand for tailored experiences that accommodate personal preferences and individual interests —on the other, heightened awareness and regulations around data privacy call for a more conscientious approach to personalization. Striking this balance involves leveraging data ethically to inform content strategy without infringing on user privacy. For example, a brand might use aggregated data to identify trends and preferences, ensuring personalized marketing efforts are based on insights rather than invasive data practices. This nuanced approach respects user privacy and enhances brand trust and loyalty.

Social Media Marketing

This encapsulates the essence of navigating the future of social media marketing. At its core, it's segmented into four quadrants, each representing a key area of focus: Trend Prediction, Platform Integration, Content Evolution, and the Privacy-Personalization Nexus. Surrounding this core, actionable strategies and examples breathe life into each quadrant, explaining the dynamic interplay of these elements. Elements, such as QR codes, links to tools for social listening, content creation resources, and privacy compliance checklists, should be explored in more detail after going through this section. This directs marketers toward strategic innovation and thoughtful engagement in the ever-changing world of social media marketing.

12.2 SUSTAINABILITY AND ETHICS IN DIGITAL MARKETING

In a world increasingly attuned to the echoes of environmental and social justice, digital marketing finds itself at a crossroads. The call for sustainability and ethical practices reverberates daily, urging brands to listen and actively respond. This shift towards ethical branding is a trend and a profound transformation in the relationship between businesses and their audiences. It encourages marketers to weave sustainability into the very fabric of their digital strategies, ensuring that every tweet, post, or campaign aligns with a greater purpose.

Promoting Sustainability

Promoting sustainability through digital marketing is more than showcasing eco-friendly products or green initiatives. It's about embedding sustainable values into every brand's digital presence. This could manifest in reducing digital carbon footprints by optimizing online content for energy efficiency or supporting and collaborating with platforms prioritizing renewable energy sources. It extends to carefully selecting partners and affiliates whose practices and ethos resonate with sustainability, creating a cohesive ecosystem that reflects the brand's commitment to the planet. Moreover, storytelling becomes a powerful tool, sharing the brand's journey towards sustainability, the challenges faced, and the victories achieved, thus inspiring both action and loyalty among audiences.

Ethical Marketing Practices

Ethical marketing practices in the digital world are built on transparency, honesty, and respect for consumer privacy. This involves a meticulous approach to data handling, where personal information is treated not as a commodity but as a sacred trust, collected and used with the utmost care and consent. Ethical practices also demand an unwavering commitment to truth in advertising. This means avoiding embellishing a product's benefits or the greenwashing of its environmental impact, ensuring that claims are accurate and verifiable. In this atmosphere, honesty becomes the cornerstone of brand-audience relationships, fostering trust and credibility.

Branding and CSR

Corporate social responsibility (CSR) initiatives offer a potent avenue for brands to amplify their ethical and sustainable values. When integrated into digital marketing strategies, CSR activities do more than bolster a brand's image; they become a testament to its values in action. This integration could take the form of digital campaigns highlighting the brand's contributions to social causes, partnerships with non-profits, or initiatives aimed at community upliftment. When communicated sincerely and without self-aggrandize, CSR initiatives resonate deeply with audiences, aligning brand values with consumer aspirations for a better world. This alignment elevates the brand's standing and cultivates a community of engaged and committed consumers.

Navigating Ethical Dilemmas

The path of ethical digital marketing is fraught with dilemmas, where the right choice is often veiled in shades of grey rather than clear-cut distinctions. Navigating these ethical quandaries demands a framework grounded in core values and guided by a steadfast moral compass. This framework should prioritize stakeholder interests, weighing the impact of marketing decisions on consumers, employees, and the broader community. It involves asking hard questions about the potential consequences of actions and ensuring that the pursuit of engagement and conversions does not come at the cost of ethical compromise. At times, it may require making difficult choices and preceding short-term gains for the integrity and long-term sustainability of the brand.

Through this rigorous process, brands safeguard their ethical standing and set a precedent, driving the industry towards higher standards of responsibility and accountability.

Sustainability and ethics in digital marketing allow brands to be called for a higher purpose. It's a call that demands more than superficial allegiance to trends or token gestures toward social causes. Instead, it asks for a deep, systemic integration of ethical practices and sustainable values into every aspect of digital marketing. From the promotion of sustainability in online content to the implementation of ethical marketing practices, the leveraging of CSR initiatives, and the navigation of moral dilemmas, the journey is complex. Yet, it promises to enhance brand reputation and consumer loyalty and contribute to the larger social and environmental stewardship group. This becomes more than a tool for brand promotion; it transforms into a platform for positive change, reflecting a brand's commitment to profitability, the planet, and its people.

12.3 ADAPTING TO NEW TECHNOLOGIES AND PLATFORMS

Adopting emerging technologies and platforms is not an option but an imperative for those aspiring to remain at the forefront of innovation. The landscape is dotted with technological advancements, each promising to redefine how brands interact with their audiences. Artificial Intelligence (AI), Augmented Reality (AR), Virtual Reality (VR), and blockchain emerge as foundations of change, illuminating pathways to unprecedented levels of engagement, personalization, and transparency. A challenge is not in the scarcity of opportunities but in discerning which technologies align with a brand's ethos and goals, ensuring their integration into marketing strategies is authentic and purposeful.

Embracing Technological Advancements

Implementing technologies like AI, AR/VR, and blockchain within marketing strategies is unavoidable if you want to stay caught up. With its ability to analyze vast datasets, AI offers insights into consumer behavior with unparalleled precision, enabling the creation of highly personalized content. Meanwhile, AR and VR invite audiences into immersive experiences that go beyond the limitations of physical space, offering a glimpse into the potential for deep, meaningful engagement. Blockchain, for its part, introduces a new paradigm of transparency and security, fostering trust in an era where skepticism towards digital entities is rampant. Exploring these technologies requires experimentation and a willingness to explore beyond the familiar boundaries of established platforms and methodologies.

Platform Diversification

The digital ecosystem is marked by its transience, platforms rising and waning with the tides of consumer preference. In this context, diversification becomes a shield, a strategy to mitigate the risks associated with over-reliance on a single platform or technology. This diversification extends beyond the presence on multiple platforms; it entails integrating various technologies to enhance the marketing mix. For instance, leveraging AI for customer service on social media platforms while experimenting with AR for product demonstrations on a brand's website. This approach ensures that a brand's digital presence is robust and capable of weathering shifts in the digital.

Skills for New Technologies

The mastery of new technologies demands a continuous investment in learning and development. The pace at which these advancements evolve renders obsolete the knowledge that once held sway. Marketers, therefore, must cultivate an environment of perpetual learning, seeking educational resources that keep pace with technological advancements. Online courses, webinars, and industry certifications become invaluable tools in this quest, offering insights into the technical aspects of these technologies and their strategic application within marketing. This dual focus on the technical and strategic enables marketers to leverage the complete potential of AI, AR/VR, and blockchain, transforming these technologies from novelties into integral components of a brand's marketing strategy.

Case Studies of Technology Adoption

Insight comes in the seat of observation, learning from those who have navigated the complexities of integrating new technologies into their marketing strategies. Consider a brand that leveraged AI to personalize its email marketing campaigns, significantly uplifting engagement and conversions. Or a retail company that employed AR to allow customers to visualize products in their homes, bridging the gap between the physical experience and online browsing.

These case studies serve as lighthouses, guiding the way through the practical challenges and opportunities emerging technologies present. They emphasize the significance of adopting a strategic approach in harmony with these technologies' capabilities and the brand's objectives and audience needs. Through these narratives, marketers gain the inspiration to innovate and the practical insights needed to navigate the implementation of new technologies.

In this exploration of adapting to new technologies and platforms, the confluence of innovation and strategy emerges as the bedrock upon which successful digital marketing is built. It is a dynamic interplay where the potential of AI, AR/VR, and blockchain is realized through thoughtful integration into marketing strategies, driven by a deep understanding of both the technologies themselves and the evolving preferences of the audience. This journey, marked by continuous learning and experimentation, has its challenges. Yet, these challenges offer the most significant rewards, propelling brands into new realms of engagement and connection with their audiences. In embracing these technologies and the diversification of platforms, marketers find the keys to unlocking new possibilities, crafting experiences that resonate deeply with consumers, and enduring in the ever-shifting landscape.

12.4 BUILDING A RESILIENT DIGITAL MARKETING BUSINESS

In this space where volatility is the norm and change is the only constant, a business's fortitude is measured not by its capacity to generate profit but by its resilience against the unforeseen storms that inevitably arise. This resilience, a multifaceted shield forged from the alloy of risk management strategies, diversification efforts, a culture that learns from missteps, and the foresight of long-term planning, becomes the cornerstone upon which sustainable growth is built.

Risk Management Strategies

Navigating the digital marketing ecosystem requires a specific approach to risk management. This process begins with identifying vulnerabilities within the business model, from operational hiccups to market fluctuations and everything in between. The subsequent phase involves:

- The development of contingency plans and detailed protocols designed to activate at the first hint of disruption.
- Ensuring that the business remains agile.
- Its operations are fluid.
- Its trajectory is mainly unaffected by external shocks.

Moreover, investing in insurance and other protective measures offers a safety net, cushioning the business from the financial impacts of unforeseen events. This strategic approach to risk management, rooted in anticipation and preparation, empowers digital marketing enterprises to navigate uncertainties confidently, turning potential threats into navigable challenges.

Diversification for Resilience

The saying about diversifying investments holds profound wisdom for digital marketing businesses seeking to build resilience. In this context, diversification is more significant than spreading assets across multiple channels; it embodies the strategic expansion of marketing strategies, revenue streams, and platforms. By cultivating a presence across a spectrum of media, from traditional blogs to the latest social media sensations, and by exploring varied revenue models, from affiliate marketing to subscription services, businesses insulate themselves against the volatility of digital trends and platform algorithms. This deliberate expansion is a wall against market shifts, ensuring that the company remains robust, its growth is steady, and its foundations are unshaken by the ebb and flow of digital trends.

Learning from Failures

Failures and setbacks are pivotal learning moments and are not a last stop; each misstep is a chapter in the broader growth narrative. Cultivating a culture that tolerates and embraces these experiences as opportunities for learning is paramount. This spirit invigorates the entire organization, encouraging experimentation and innovation while mitigating the fear of failure that often stifles creativity. Analyzing campaigns that fell short of their objectives, dissecting the factors that led to their underperformance, and extracting actionable insights become standard practice. This reflective process transforms setbacks into stepping stones, each failure a lesson that refines strategies, sharpens skills and fortifies the business against future challenges.

Long-term Planning

Amidst the whirlwind of day-to-day operations and the allure of short-term gains, the importance of long-term planning in building a resilient digital marketing business cannot be overstated. This strategic foresight involves setting a vision that extends beyond the immediate horizon, mapping out a route that navigates through anticipated market developments, technological advancements, and shifts in consumer behavior. It requires a steadfast commitment to this vision, tempered by the flexibility to adapt plans as new information and opportunities arise. Long-term planning also underscores the necessity of sustainable practices, ensuring that growth strategies align with ethical standards and contribute positively to the broader community. Through this lens, long-term planning becomes the compass that guides the business, not solely towards profitability but towards enduring significance and impact in the digital marketing reality.

In weaving together these threads of resilience—risk management, diversification, learning from failures, and long-term planning—a digital marketing business not only secures its place in the present landscape but also charts a course for sustainable success in the future. This resilient foundation enables the company to weather the storms of uncertainty, adapt to the shifting sands of digital trends, and emerge not just untouched but stronger, ready to seize new opportunities and continue its ascent in the ever-evolving world of digital marketing.

12.5 LEAVING A LEGACY THROUGH DIGITAL INFLUENCE

In the interconnected web of digital marketing, legacy transcends the mere accumulation of metrics, aiming instead for a lasting imprint on the fabric of the industry and its audience. This vision compels us to not only strive for success in the present but to cast our sights on the enduring impact of our actions, shaping the landscape for generations of marketers to come. Crafting a brand that resonates through time, inspiring future visionaries, contributing to the sector's expansion, and making a tangible difference in society encapsulates the essence of a legacy beyond sole business accomplishments.

Strategies for constructing a digital marketing brand with lasting influence involve a meticulous blend of authenticity, innovation, and community engagement. Authenticity ensures that the brand's core values are communicated and lived, creating a genuine connection with audiences that withstands the test of time. Innovation keeps the brand as the main focus of digital marketing advancements, continually evolving to meet changing consumer needs and technological landscapes. Meanwhile, community engagement fosters a sense of belonging and loyalty among consumers, encouraging active participation in the brand's journey. These elements, woven together, form the foundation of a brand destined to leave a mark on the industry and its audience long after specific campaigns have faded from memory.

Inspiring the next generation of digital marketers involves more than imparting wisdom—it's about igniting a passion for the field's boundless possibilities. Through mentorship, thought leadership, and the setting of positive examples, we pave the way for emerging talents, offering them a canvas upon which to sketch their visions. Mentorship programs provide a direct channel to share knowledge and experience, guiding novices through the complexities of digital marketing with a steady hand. Thought leadership, expressed through blogs, speaking engagements, and social media, challenges conventional thinking and introduces fresh perspectives, stirring a creative ferment in the minds of up-and-comers. By demonstrating ethical practices, innovative strategies, and a commitment to continuous learning, we set a standard for the industry, inspiring others to strive for excellence and integrity in their endeavors.

Contributing to the industry's growth encapsulates a drive for personal or organizational success and a broader vision for digital marketing's future. We fuel the sector's evolution through collaboration, innovation, and knowledge sharing, pushing the boundaries of what's possible. Collaborative projects and partnerships with other organizations foster a culture of innovation, leveraging diverse talents and perspectives to tackle challenges and seize opportunities. Sharing knowledge through industry publications, forums, or conferences enriches the collective understanding, elevating the entire field. This commitment to the industry's advancement ensures that digital marketing remains a dynamic and vibrant discipline, capable of adapting to an ever-changing world.

Understanding the social impact of our work in digital marketing invites a reflection on the broader consequences of our strategies and campaigns. It's about recognizing our power to influence societal norms, behaviors, and values through the content we create and the messages we amplify. This awareness compels us to wield that power responsibly, championing causes that resonate with our values and contributing to positive change. Campaigns highlighting social issues promote sustainability or support community initiatives to bolster the brand's image and make a tangible difference in the world. This intersection of digital marketing and social responsibility embodies the essence of a legacy that transcends business success, marking our contributions to a world that is better for our efforts.

In creating this evolution of lasting influence, our endeavors in digital marketing become more than a pursuit of success; they transform into a journey for significance. Crafting a brand that endures, inspiring future leaders, fostering industry growth, and making a positive societal impact encapsulate the vision of a legacy that reaches beyond the confines of our careers. It's a legacy that contributes to shaping the digital marketing landscape, ensuring that our efforts resonate not just today but in the narratives of tomorrow.

As we close this chapter, we reflect on the journey of creating a legacy in the digital environment. Our efforts in building enduring brands, mentoring the next generation, catalyzing industry growth, and impacting society lay the foundation for a legacy beyond mere business achievements. This vision for a lasting influence elevates our work today and shapes the future of digital marketing, inspiring innovation, integrity, and positive change in the chapters to come.

CONCLUSION

Look at that; you made it! You understood the foundation of the digital nomad mindset to learn about the advancements of digital marketing strategies. We've navigated the evolution from foundational concepts to present-day techniques. We've unpacked the critical importance of niche selection, the art of crafting a compelling personal brand, and the magic of leveraging social media for exponential growth. We've clarified the power of SEO and explored the multiple ways to monetize digital platforms. From managing multiple income streams to the base requirement of continuous learning and why it's essential, we've covered a lot of ground.

At the heart of it all, adaptability is the foundation of your path to success. Embracing change, experimenting with new platforms and strategies, and being ready to pivot based on market and technological advancements is the essence of thriving in digital marketing.

Now, I urge you to take that bold first step. Just take action —maybe an area you're comfortable with or one that's sparked your interest for a while. Then, let your curiosity lead you to expand your skills, strategies, and, most importantly, your mindset! Remember, the digital marketing universe is vast and filled with opportunities waiting for you to take them.

I've walked this path, faced the trials, celebrated the triumphs, and I'm here to tell you: yes, it's challenging, but oh, it's incredibly rewarding. The sense of accomplishment you feel after each win, no matter how big or small. It's time to create your aspirations for financial independence and autonomy and live that digital nomad lifestyle that you've dreamed of.

Stay curious. Keep up with the latest trends and technologies. Follow the leaders in digital marketing, join workshops, and immerse yourself in online communities. Do not be afraid to put yourself out there and to have humility. It's your golden ticket to staying ahead of the curve and achieving lasting success. Share your journey, seek advice, and connect with other marketers. You never know what you can learn. Please always remember to be coachable and teachable, and you will remain in a good spot of continuous self-growth.

Thank you, truly, for coming on this ride with me. Your drive, dreams, and dedication to mastering a more meaningful lifestyle have inspired every page of this book. I can't wait to hear about your successes, learnings, and even the stumbling blocks you turn into stepping stones.

As we part ways, I leave you with this: Step into the life you're creating with the skills and knowledge that are now within you. Always be your true, authentic self, and let your story unfold naturally. The online world is literally at your fingertips, and the opportunities are endless.

Here's to your success, freedom, and many more flights to take.

Yours in this journey, Amelia

Keeping the Game Alive

Now, you have everything you need to Master Digital Marketing; it's time to pass on your newfound knowledge and show other readers where they can find the same help.

Simply by leaving your honest opinion of this book on Amazon, you'll show other Online Marketers where they can find the information they're looking for and pass on your passion for Online Marketing.

I appreciate your help. The Digital Marketing space thrives when we pass on our knowledge, and you're helping me to do just that.

Scan the QR code below to leave a review:

REFERENCES

- Smart Insights. (2023). *2024 Digital marketing trends shaping the future of marketing.* Retrieved from https://www.smartinsights.com/digital-marketing-strategy/digital-strategy-development/digital-marketing-trends-2024/
- LinkedIn. (2023). *2023 case studies of successful digital marketing campaigns.* Retrieved from https://www.linkedin.com/pulse/2023-case-studies-successful-digital-marketing-campaigns-nb2jf
- Marketing Insider Group. (n.d.). *The 10 best digital marketing tools for small businesses.* Retrieved from https://marketinginsidergroup.com/content-marketing/best-digital-marketing-tools-for-small-businesses/
- Two Rivers Marketing. (2023). *Data privacy: What marketers need to know in 2024 and beyond.* Retrieved from https://www.tworiversmarketing.com/blog/data-privacy-what-marketers-need-to-know-in-2024-and-beyond
- LinkedIn. (n.d.). *How to conduct market research in a niche market.* Retrieved from https://www.linkedin.com/advice/1/what-unique-considerations-when-conducting-market-research-34m9c
- Mirasee. (2024). *15 winning niche market examples (updated for 2024).* Retrieved from https://mirasee.com/blog/niche-market-examples/
- Exploding Topics. (2024). *11 top market analysis tools (2024).* Retrieved from https://explodingtopics.com/blog/market-analysis-tools
- Vitasek, K. (2023, April 10). *How passion and purpose are driving forces within successful collaborations.* Forbes. Retrieved from https://www.forbes.com/sites/katevitasek/2023/04/10/how-passion-and-purpose-are-driving-forces-within-successful-collaborations/
- Harvard Business Review. (2023, May). *A new approach to building your personal brand.* Retrieved from https://hbr.org/2023/05/a-new-approach-to-building-your-personal-brand
- Buffer. (2024). *23 top social media sites for your brand in 2024, ranked.* Retrieved from https://buffer.com/library/social-media-sites/

- SEMrush. (n.d.). *The ultimate guide to creating a content marketing strategy*. Retrieved from https://www.semrush.com/blog/content-marketing-strategy-guide/
- RedAlkemi. (n.d.). *Leveraging influencer partnerships for brand growth*. Retrieved from https://www.redalkemi.com/blog/influencer-marketing-leveraging-influencer-partnerships-for-brand-growth
- Backlinko. (n.d.). *SEO trends in 2024 and how to adapt*. Retrieved from https://backlinko.com/seo-this-year
- OptinMonster. (n.d.). *11 web design principles that can boost your conversion rate*. Retrieved from https://optinmonster.com/11-web-design-principles-that-will-boost-your-conversion-rate/
- Forbes. (2024, March). *Best SEO tools & software*. Retrieved from https://www.forbes.com/advisor/business/software/best-seo-software/
- LocaliQ. (n.d.). *7 real-world SEO examples to learn from*. Retrieved from https://localiq.com/blog/seo-examples/
- SEMrush. (n.d.). *7 marketing trends to watch in 2024 (+ tips and examples)*. Retrieved from https://www.semrush.com/blog/marketing-trends/
- HubSpot. (n.d.). *11 Facebook case studies & success stories to inspire you*. Retrieved from https://blog.hubspot.com/marketing/facebook-case-study
- The Boss Magazine. (n.d.). *The impact of social media influencers on apparel brand growth*. Retrieved from https://thebossmagazine.com/impact-social-media-influencers-apparel-brand-growth/
- Hootsuite. (n.d.). *How to plan a winning cross-platform campaign*. Retrieved from https://blog.hootsuite.com/cross-platform-campaign/
- KORONA POS. (n.d.). *10 eCommerce social media marketing success case studies*. Retrieved from https://koronapos.com/blog/social-media-marketing-case-studies/
- Hootsuite. (2024). *How to build a social media growth strategy that works*. Retrieved from https://blog.hootsuite.com/social-media-growth/
- Authority Hacker. (2024). *13 best influencer affiliate programs & networks in 2024*. Retrieved from https://www.authorityhacker.com/influencer-affiliate-programs/
- Easy Digital Downloads. (n.d.). *How to increase digital sales with social media (best tips)*. Retrieved from https://easydigitaldownloads.com/blog/use-social-media-effectively-for-digital-product-store/

- Moosend. (n.d.). *11 effective email marketing strategies for 2024.* Retrieved from https://moosend.com/blog/email-marketing-strategies/
- Backlinko. (2024). *19 new SEO techniques [2024 update].* Retrieved from https://backlinko.com/seo-techniques
- Protocol 80. (n.d.). *18 uplifting PPC statistics & success stories for small businesses.* Retrieved from https://www.protocol80.com/blog/ppc-statistics-small-business
- HubSpot. (n.d.). *Conversion rate optimization (CRO): 8 ways to get started.* Retrieved from https://blog.hubspot.com/marketing/conversion-rate-optimization-guide
- Leadfeeder. (n.d.). *The best 37 marketing automation tools to use in 2024.* Retrieved from https://www.leadfeeder.com/blog/marketing-automation-tools/
- ClickUp. (n.d.). *8 steps to scale your content production process.* Retrieved from https://clickup.com/blog/content-production-scaling/
- DigitalOcean. (n.d.). *28 best practices for managing remote teams.* Retrieved from https://www.digitalocean.com/resources/article/managing-remote-teams
- NetSuite. (n.d.). *4 steps to creating a financial plan for your small business.* Retrieved from https://www.netsuite.com/portal/resource/articles/financial-management/small-business-financial-plan.shtml
- Bankrate. (n.d.). *25 passive income ideas to help you make money in 2024.* Retrieved from https://www.bankrate.com/investing/passive-income-ideas/
- Ahrefs. (n.d.). *Affiliate marketing for beginners: What it is + how to.* Retrieved from https://ahrefs.com/blog/affiliate-marketing/
- Mighty Networks. (n.d.). *11 best platforms to sell online courses in 2024.* Retrieved from https://www.mightynetworks.com/resources/best-platform-to-sell-courses-online
- Thinkific. (n.d.). *Digital product pricing strategy.* Retrieved from https://www.thinkific.com/blog/digital-product-pricing-strategy/
- eSoftSkills. (n.d.). *Cost reduction strategies through automation.* Retrieved from https://esoftskills.com/dm/cost-reduction-strategies-through-automation/
- Harvard Business Review. (2012). *Making advanced analytics work for you.* Retrieved from https://hbr.org/2012/10/making-advanced-analytics-work-for-you

- BizBuySell. (n.d.). *How to value and sell your website or e-commerce business*. Retrieved from https://www.bizbuysell.com/learning-center/guide/sell-ecommerce-business/
- Medium. (n.d.). *10 effective time management techniques for digital nomads: How to work smarter and travel more*. Retrieved from https://medium.com/@jayrald.ado/10-effective-time-management-techniques-for-digital-nomads-how-to-work-smarter-and-travel-more-5adc1dc9394a
- Retail Week Connect. (n.d.). *How to cope with information overload as a marketer*. Retrieved from https://retail-week-connect.com/how-to-cope-with-information-overload-as-a-marketer/
- Forbes Business Council. (2022, July 25). *7 ways to stand out and thrive in a saturated market*. Forbes. Retrieved from https://www.forbes.com/sites/forbesbusinesscouncil/2022/07/25/7-ways-to-stand-out-and-thrive-in-a-saturated-market/
- Sprout Social. (n.d.). *Everything you need to know about social media algorithms*. Retrieved from https://sproutsocial.com/insights/social-media-algorithms/
- Break the Ice Media. (n.d.). *Mindsets & marketing: Embracing a growth mindset*. Retrieved from https://breaktheicemedia.com/mindsets-marketing-how-embracing-a-growth-mindset-can-set-your-destination-up-for-success/
- HBS Online. (n.d.). *Networking for entrepreneurs: 5 tips & strategies*. Retrieved from https://online.hbs.edu/blog/post/networking-for-entrepreneurs
- Smart Insights. (2024). *2024 digital marketing trends shaping the future of marketing*. Retrieved from https://www.smartinsights.com/digital-marketing-strategy/digital-strategy-development/digital-marketing-trends-2024/
- HBS Online. (n.d.). *How to create a digital marketing plan: 4 steps*. Retrieved from https://online.hbs.edu/blog/post/digital-marketing-plan
- Peaberry Web. (n.d.). *WordPress services*. Retrieved from https://peaberryweb.com/wordpress-services/
- GlowHost Forums. (n.d.). *What is ethical SEO?*. Retrieved from https://forums.glowhost.com/search-engines-talk/what-ethical-search-engine-optimization-5498.html#post29138
- SolidPixels Academy. (n.d.). *SEO writing missteps: What not to do for search engine success*. Retrieved from https://academy.solidpixels.com/en/blog/seo-writing-missteps-what-not-to-do-for-search-engine-success

- Dreamwright. (n.d.). *10 essential strategies when SEO is good but conversions are bad*. Retrieved from https://dreamwright.com/10-essential-strategies-when-seo-is-good-but-conversions-are-bad/
- Cboomarank. (n.d.). *Black hat SEO and white hat SEO: What's the difference?*. Retrieved from https://www.cboomarank.com/black-hat-seo-and-white-hat-seo/
- Muon Marketing. (n.d.). *Is local SEO worth it in Ohio?*. Retrieved from https://muonmarketing.com/blogs/is-local-seo-worth-it-in-ohio/
- DDG Office. (n.d.). *The future of SEO and SMM*. Retrieved from https://ddgoffice.com/the-future-of-seo-and-smm/
- COO Science. (n.d.). *Choosing the right social media platforms for your brand*. Retrieved from https://coo.science/choosing-the-right-social-media-platforms-for-your-brand/
- COSEOM. (n.d.). *The 8 leading B2B social media trends of 2024*. Retrieved from https://www.coseom.com/b2b-social-media-trends-2024/
- Pcsoftnepal. (n.d.). *The art of crafting compelling calls-to-action*. Retrieved from https://pcsoftnepal.com/blog/our-blog-1/the-art-of-crafting-compelling-calls-to-action-3
- M&G Marketing. (n.d.). *Unleash your PPC career: Essential guide*. Retrieved from https://speed.cy/ppc-management/the-essential-guide-to-a-career-as-a-ppc-specialist
- My Marketing Efforts Will Dominate Your Face. (n.d.). *What are the steps of conversion optimization*. Retrieved from https://www.mymarketingeffortswilldominateyourface.com/what-are-the-steps-of-conversion-optimization
- GTS. (n.d.). *How to conduct A/B testing for marketing campaigns?*. Retrieved from https://www.gandhitechnoweb.com/p/blog/how-to-conduct-a-b-testing-for-marketing-campaigns/
- Simple Website Profits. (n.d.). *5 proven strategies for implementing affiliate links on your website*. Retrieved from https://simplewebsiteprofits.com/how-to-put-affiliate-links-on-your-website/